No Sacrifice
Too Great

No Sacrifice Too Great

CT Studd, From Cricket Field to Mission Field

Gordon Pettie

Sovereign World

Published by Sovereign World Ltd
Ellel Grange, Bay Horse, Lancaster, Lancashire LA2 0HN
www.sovereignworld.com
Facebook: www.facebook.com/sovereignworld

ISBN 978-1-85240-8589 (Printed edition)
ISBN 978-1 85240-8596 (EBook)

Printed in Great Britain by Bell and Bain Ltd, Glasgow

British Library Cataloguing-in-Publication Data.
A catalogue record for this book is available from the British Library.

Only one life, yes only one,
Now let me say: 'Thy will be done.'
And when at last I'll hear the call,
I know I'll say: 't'was worth it all.'
Only one life, 'twill soon be past,
Only what's done for Christ will last.
C T Studd

Contents

Foreword

I am so glad that Gordon Pettie has written this brilliant new biography of 'C T Studd', or just CT, as he was popularly known. His story is one of the most outstanding missionary stories of the nineteenth and twentieth centuries, which every subsequent generation of believers needs to read, with thanksgiving, admiration, and even awe, such was CT's perseverance against all odds.

You won't find any wishy-washy obedience in CT's story. He firmly believed that if God had called you, then God knew what He was doing. This belief underpinned his entire life and fuelled his determination to never give up on what God had asked him to do, no matter what the cost, hardship or personal sacrifice.

In this very well researched book, Gordon graphically portrays how CT's gritty determination was anchored in the sure call of God for the whole of his life. As a young man CT gave up a glittering cricket career to follow Jesus to the ends of the earth.

This call of God first took him to China, then to India and finally to the Belgian Congo in Africa, where he died.

In the book, Gordon courageously looks at some of the personal relationship difficulties that were a consequence of CT's single-mindedness in the pursuit of his calling. Determined people are not always the easiest of people to relate with – as has been observed throughout Christian history from the Apostle Paul onwards!

I am personally passionate about the Studd family story. The three Studd brothers, and their parents, were all converted through the ministry of the most famous nineteenth century evangelist, D L Moody. It was through CT's oldest brother, Kynaston, that my mother met my father. I wouldn't exist today were it not for D L Moody and the Studd family!

I pray that this new biography of CT will reach and inspire a new generation of believers, especially those who are unfamiliar with this giant of faith – a giant who, wherever he put down his feet for the Lord, saw God open up the way, even in the face of seemingly impossible difficulties. His footprints stride across China, India and Africa and the legacy of his life today still grows, with ever-increasing fruit for the Kingdom of God through the ongoing work of Worldwide Evangelisation for Christ (WEC) International.

The amazing collection of photographs which Gordon uses to illustrate the book feed the imagination and bring visual understanding of the reality of life for CT and his family in these far flung nations. They give reality and understanding of just how great a man CT was.

When I heard that Gordon Pettie was writing a new biography of CT, and his wife Priscilla, for a new generation, my heart leapt. There could not be a better person to write such an intimate and challenging biography. It has been a privilege to know Gordon for many years and experience first hand his own dedication in the service of the Lord. The Body of Christ will be grateful to Gordon for accepting the challenge of chronicling the life of CT in such a fresh, new and challenging way.

I will be recommending this book wherever I go. I believe it will be a classic of missionary biography – essential reading for all those who want their lives to really count for the Kingdom of God.

Peter Horrobin
Founder of Ellel Ministries International

Preface

A note arrived on my desk asking me to ring a *Revelation TV* viewer. When I rang the number, a dear 94-year-old lady answered. She told me she'd started clearing the attic of her house and had come across what she described as a first edition book on Hudson Taylor and the work of the China Inland Mission. Since she knew that I had recently written a book featuring the life of Hudson Taylor,[1] she wondered if I would like it. Like it? I jumped at the generous offer that she was making and told her I would be honoured to receive the book.

However, there was just one problem. She considered the book was too precious to send through the post. If I wanted it I would have to arrange for someone to collect it from her.

I checked where the viewer lived and noted that two members of the *Revelation* team lived approximately an hour and a half from her. I explained the situation to them and they agreed to collect the book for me.

Several days later, I received another phone call. This time it was from the team member who had gone to collect the book. He explained that he had visited the viewer that day but there was no book! Only a collection of papers, dating back to 1885, and the valedictory meetings in Cambridge, Oxford and London of a group of university students. These young men had committed their lives to serving the Lord in China with Hudson Taylor and the China Inland Mission, and were known at the time as the Cambridge Seven.

I was intrigued. What had I been given?

A few days later the papers were in my possession. To be honest I was more excited to receive them than if there had been a first edition book which might have been worth considerable money. How I wish I could describe them to you. Twenty pages of closely-knit print. A little faded. The heading was 'China's Millions,' edited by J Hudson Taylor, dated March 1885, number 3, and priced at one penny. There was a note on the front page which told readers they could have the China Inland Mission's newsletter by post for a full year for 1s 6d!

But it was the content that thrilled me. This was a report of the evangelistic tour that preceded a group of seven young students leaving for China. Their decision to leave good careers in politics, business and the military, to go and preach the gospel in faraway China, had become national news. The British secular press had dubbed them the Cambridge Seven.

Within that group of students, the most well-known was a gentleman called Charles T Studd. He was famous for his achievements on the cricket field, and was considered the finest all-round cricketer England had ever produced.

The magazine recorded the words Charles T Studd shared with

an audience in the Exeter Hall, London on the 4 February 1885. It was the night before he, William Cassels, Stanley P Smith, Dixon E Hoste, Montagu Beauchamp, Cecil Polhill-Turner and Arthur T Polhill-Turner, departed for China.

The magazine described how so many tried to attend the meeting that it became 'a living mass of human beings.' An overflow meeting was hurriedly arranged in the Lower Hall, and even then, many were turned away. The *Nonconformist* newspaper of the day, wrote: 'Never before, probably in the history of mission, has so unique a band, set out to labour in the foreign field, as the one that stood last night on the platform of Exeter Hall.'[2]

When Charles Studd stood up to speak, he began with the words:

'I want to recommend you tonight to my Master. I have tried many ways of pleasure in my time; I have been running after the best Master, and thank God, by His grace I have found Him. I wish to tell you how the Lord has sought and found me, and how He has led me back to himself.'

I was intrigued by his story and began to read all that I could find about him and the Cambridge Seven.

Charles Studd decided to leave the luxury of English country life, and the fame his cricket had brought him, giving away his inherited fortune worth millions in today's money. His life saw enormous blessing and sacrifice. Christian missions have spawned out of his labours and still attract thousands to work in them today. Without a doubt, Charles Studd was a radical, who was not afraid to say things as they were and, towards the end of his life, became a controversial figure.

His story – and this book – is an urgent cry to Christians today to wake out of their lethargy and share Christ with an increasingly lost and hurting world. Are you ready for the challenge?

Charles Studd left virtually no written record of his life. His mother and wife did the next best thing; they preserved all his correspondence from boyhood. Then Charles's son-in law, Norman Grubb, who took over leadership of the work his father-in-law started and saw it grow significantly during his time in charge, took that correspondence and his own life's experiences working alongside Charles and wrote the nearest thing to an autobiography of Charles Studd's life.

One of the hardest parts of writing a biography of someone who lived a hundred years ago, is accuracy. Take something as simple as the inheritance that Charles Studd received when his father died. Did he receive it when he was 25 or 26? Both ages are mentioned in different biographies. At the time of reaching the age when his inheritance was due, Charles Studd was in the Chinese city of Chungking. Who sent the package of papers and documents with details of the inheritance to him? Was it the family solicitors, or was it the family bankers? Some biographers say solicitors but the firm's name of 'Coutts' sounds remarkably like the well-known bank. Once Charles had received the documents, he appointed a power of attorney to handle his affairs. Did he appoint the family solicitors, family bankers or his brother Kynaston? All are suggested in different books.

You may ask if it really matters. Christians like to present a happy, positive account of people's lives and witness. Sometimes that means the stories we read are not accurate. Believe me, I have tried to be factually correct. It is an important principle if we are to live Christ-like lives. When God creates history, he does it through the lives of individuals. That is what I have sought to do in this book.

PREFACE

I am very grateful for the help that I have received as I have researched the life of Charles Studd, his wife, Priscilla, and the work of the China Inland Mission (now known as Overseas Missionary Fellowship) and WEC International. I especially want to thank Marion Osgood, the archivist for the China Inland Mission/OMF International (UK), and Fiona Adams, the International Archive Co-ordinator for WEC International, for their help. The cover was designed by my good friend Craig Stock, and he also helped with photographs in the book, as did Chrissie Brown from WEC International. I have never had an editor before, 'Thank you Michele (Hackney)' for guiding me through the process, and the same to Rosalinde Joosten at Sovereign World Publishing. Finally my beloved wife, Lorna! How can I thank her enough for putting up with me spending hours at my desk, or in coffee shops, as I researched and wrote. Love you all and thank you.

One of those who worked alongside Charles Studd in Africa was Alfred Buxton. In time he became his son-in-law. He accompanied Charles on his first trip to Africa and laboured in the new mission work his father-in-law established. Sadly, Charles fell out with him and dismissed him from the Mission. Even so Alfred wrote the foreword for Norman Grubb's epic book *CT Studd, Athlete and Pioneer*, describing him in this way:

> CT's life stands as some rugged Gibraltar – a sign to all
> succeeding generations that it is worthwhile to lose all
> this world can offer and stake everything on the world
> to come. His life will be an eternal rebuke to easy-going
> Christianity. He has demonstrated what it means to follow
> Christ without counting the cost and without looking
> back.

> CT was essentially a cavalry leader … A cavalry leader cannot have all the gifts of an administrator, or he would not have the qualities to lead a charge. In this simple fact is the explanation of the shortcomings some might point out. If there were these, they were in reality the exaggeration of CT's unique qualities: His courage in an emergency, his determination never to sound the retreat, his conviction that he was in God's will, his faith that God would see him through, his contempt of the arm of the flesh, and his willingness to risk all for Christ.[3]

My longing as you read this story, is that you will look beyond the lives of Charles and his wife Priscilla, their children, the Cambridge Seven, the workers on the mission fields, and those serving at home, to the Saviour they all loved and longed to introduce to a lost and dying world. Our world is a very different world to the world of the early 1900s, but spiritually only the Saviour they served can satisfy people's lives.

As I am writing this manuscript, I am reading the latest book from George Verwer, the founder of Operation Mobilisation.[4] He has a great quote in his book, in which he says, 'Every organisation or institution in all of history … has proven that *where two or three people are gathered together, there will be a mess*' (my italic).

There will be times as you read this story that you will come across mess! But don't let the mess put you off what Charles and Priscilla – or CT and Priscilla as I refer to them – achieved in their lifetime … and don't let mess in your own life stop you from following their example and serving the Master they served, and His kingdom.

Gordon Pettie, May 2022

Introduction

It was February 1928. CT was sixty-seven and his wife sixty-three. Although they were still husband and wife, neither had seen the other for twelve years. They had four children and lots of grandchildren and were still busy running a fast-growing mission; but she was living in the UK and he in the Belgian Congo. Britain had post and telephone boxes but such facilities had not yet reached Africa. Neither had heard the other's voice, or spoken to the other in all that time. Their only means of communication was by 'snail-mail' between the UK and the Congo.

Whenever it had been suggested to CT during those twelve years that he return to the UK for a sabbatical and to be with his wife, to have some of his ailments treated, to meet the mission supporters, or simply to have a rest, he was always adamant that he would not do so. If the idea was raised of his wife, Priscilla, or 'Scilla' as she was affectionately known, coming to visit him in the Congo, he always gave reasons why she must not do so. He really believed that the heat and lifestyle would kill her. Now, however, an opportunity had come for Scilla to visit him, and he could not think of any reasons why he should say no.

Priscilla had been travelling with a friend through the Mediterranean and had landed in Egypt. The distance from Egypt to the Congo was not too far. When the idea was raised, CT said it was out of the question for him to go to Egypt. However, with the building of roads by the Belgium government, it was realised that Priscilla could reach CT in a matter of days, after leaving Rejaf on the Nile. So it was agreed. After all the years that Priscilla had been promoting the Mission throughout the United Kingdom, Australia, America and Canada, now she was to see it for herself. But even more important, she would see her beloved CT again. It was not spoken about, but both CT and Priscilla understood, even before they met, that it would be their one and only meeting this side of heaven.

When news leaked out to the African's that *Mama Bwana* (as they called her) was coming to visit, there was great excitement. For CT there was a degree of nervousness. The last time he had seen her, he was waving out of the 9.40 am train window, as it pulled out of Paddington station on the 24 July 1916, as he departed for Africa. Now she was on her way to see him, and to see the work and meet the people. He wondered if the spark, the passion, the romance they had once had, would still be there. Their love letters from all those years ago, showed that there was real love when they had first married. But that was a long time ago. And what about the tensions and disputes that were simmering below the surface of the Mission?

The African drums let him know her progress as she drew nearer and nearer to him at Ibambi, in the Congo. The people (estimated at over 2000 in number) gathered very excitedly to see her. They began to cheer as her arrival drew near. Then there she was in front of him ... in front of them.

When formal introductions to the local dignitaries who had gathered to greet her had been carried out, CT gently guided his wife to his bamboo house so that they could have private time together. There was so much to catch up on. CT was amazed at how well she looked for her nearly sixty-four years. He could still see the beauty that was there all those years ago when he first saw her in Shanghai. Her golden hair had turned grey, but her blue eyes sparkled. The Irish lilt in her voice, gained through her upbringing in Lisburn, Northern Ireland, had not been lost over the years.

However, Priscilla could not say the same about her beloved CT. He was only four years older than her, yet walked with a stoop and the African sun had shrivelled his skin. Sickness was all about him with swelling to his hands and feet, a heart problem, enlarged liver, congested lungs, and so the list went on. As for his clothing? Oh dear. They were twenty-year hand-downs. CT had no interest in possessions of any kind, including what he wore and he was not going to change, even for his wife coming to see him. She was too polite to criticise his appearance and they settled down opposite one another to talk.

When a husband and wife meet for the first time in twelve years, what do they talk about? Priscilla wanted to fill him in on the news of the family and especially their four girls.

The Africans had always been told that their *Mama Bwana* was at home, so busy getting white men and women to come out and tell them about Jesus, that she could not come herself. But when they saw her in person they began to understand the sacrifice that

CT and his wife had made to bring salvation to them. She spoke (through an interpreter) on several occasions during the thirteen days that she was with them and they fell in love with her. Priscilla also met the Mission team, many of whom she knew personally as they had stayed at the Mission headquarters before journeying out to the Congo. There was so much to do, so many people to meet and so many places CT wanted to show her.

Priscilla's role as head of the Mission in the UK had not been an easy one, and the hardest part had been dealing with CT himself. She could see that the Home Committee and CT were heading for an almighty showdown, if she could not reach reconciliation. The couple therefore used some of their private times to try to deal with some of the issues.

One of these was the Christian pamphlet that CT had written with the words *I Don't Care a Dam* as the title and a skull and cross bones on the front. Priscilla was dismayed that he had done such a thing and the Committee had refused to publish it. CT could not understand this reaction and, when challenged, responded triumphantly that 'When they refused to print it, I had the pamphlet printed privately.'

On another occasion Priscilla raised the question of CT's drug taking which had become a real issue in the UK, with supporters questioning what was going on. CT could not understand what the fuss was about. He had always acted as his own doctor, administering drugs, mainly morphine, to deal with the pain of gallstones, heart, malaria and whatever else was attacking him. He did it quite openly and somehow news had reached back to the UK. Indeed, maybe it was CT himself who, quite innocently, had passed the information on. In one of his letters to Scilla he wrote:

God works in wonderful ways. I was bad with fever and
in bed with a temperature of 102.6. Crowds came, so I
gave myself an injection of morphine. I went out, took
the meeting which lasted five hours or more, came back
smiling with no temperature at all … People are getting
right with God at considerable sacrifice.[1]

All too soon, after only thirteen days, Priscilla's visit was over.
That was all the time she spent with CT in the last thirteen years
of their married life. Charles wrote of their time together:

She came. Once again, I marvelled at the way God used her
to speak to the natives. She seemed to know all about them
and to speak to their very hearts. I have reason to know that
few, if any, ever forgot her words. It was a joy to be on the
same platform with her again, but her presence was an agony
to me all the time, for plainly I could see the terrible cost to
her of every day, yea hour, that she spent here.

She pleaded with me to be allowed to stay; she almost
became rebellious, and then how she prayed that I would
go home with her, and assured me that the work would go
on just the same here; but there is never any doubt in one's
mind when the real word of command from God comes.

That command came to me, and it was: 'Stay.'

And so it was that we parted.[2]

The parting was terrible. CT and Priscilla said goodbye to each
other in the privacy of his bamboo house, knowing it was the last
time they would ever be together. They prayed for each other, and
asked God's blessing on the work and children and grand-children.
Then slowly they walked, arm in arm, to a waiting motor car
down the path from the house, without another word being said.

The watching crowd sensed the solemnity of the occasion and stood silent, taking it all in. The car door was opened. Priscilla got in with set face and eyes straight ahead in front of her and was driven away.

During Priscilla's brief visit, they had covered so many years. They reminisced about their times in China, as well as in India. CT reminded her that they served a God who supplied every need, and He had done just that. They looked back at the miracle of acquiring the property in Highland Road, London, as their living accommodation and Mission headquarters. Such memories. Neither of them had many more years left on earth before they were called home by their Saviour. But what a story they had to tell.

CHAPTER 1

The Early Years

Pater Familias

Charles Studd's father, Edward Studd, was born in Bombay on Christmas Day 1819. He was a successful businessman who owned two indigo plantations in Bihar, northern India. The indigo dye was extracted from tropical plants as a fermented leaf solution. It was then mixed with lye, pressed into cakes and produced in powder form. This was a time when indigo was big business, since it was the only blue dye available in the world, and life was wonderful for Edward. In January 1846, he had married a lovely lady in Calcutta, by the name of Henrietta Margaret Hudson. Sadly she died seven years later, but not before she had given birth to four children: Henrietta Margaret, Edward John Charles, Henry Malden, and Emily Adeline.

After the death of his first wife, Edward decided to sell up and move to England. The sale of the property and plantations made him a very wealthy man. Three years later he married

Dorothy (Dora) Sophia Thomas, who came from a wealthy Bedfordshire family. To Dora and Edward more children arrived – John Edward Kynaston, George Brown, Charles Thomas (CT), Arthur Haythorne, Dora Sophia, Herbert William and Reginald Augustus. Between his two wives Edward fathered eleven children.

Charles Thomas Studd was born in England on 2 December 1860. His father, by this time, had acquired extensive property interests, owning Hallerton Hall in Leicestershire and later taking a lease on a large country house in Tedworth (later changed to Tidworth), near Andover, Wiltshire. Tedworth House was everything you would imagine a grand country house to be. It had an imposing exterior, with huge white columns, and its own extensive grounds and parkland. It had expensive furnishings, beautiful décor, maids scurrying around dusting and sweeping, and elegantly proportioned rooms set around a fan shaped staircase and magnificent hall. There was also a town house in the fashionable Hyde Park Gardens in the centre of London.

To while away his time Edward took to the traditional gentleman pursuits of his day, becoming a keen huntsman and a master of hounds in Leicestershire. He loved playing cards, attending the theatre and had a passion for horse racing. Within the Tedworth House grounds he built and ran his own racecourse with extensive stables. These housed twenty of the finest race horses of the day and they also had some of the highest standards in caring and training horses.

The pinnacle of Edward's success as a horse trainer was when he won the 1866 Aintree Grand National with a horse called *Salamander*, priced at 40-1. Another of his horses, *Despatch*, gave him further success when it came second in the 1871 Grand National. Unfortunately *Salamander* later fell and had to be destroyed, an occasion which the Studd family marked by dressing in black at dinner.

The wealth brought for Charles and his brothers and sisters, great privileges. These were the days when country-house cricket was at its height and one of the paddocks was turned into a first-class cricket ground. The children received the best education, with the boys attending Eton and the assumption that they would progress on to university – Cambridge being the university of choice.

Conversions

In 1877 one of Edward's best friends, a Mr Vincent who was also a wealthy retired indigo planter, went to Ireland to watch the famous Irish Derby. After the race he rushed to Kingstown harbour to catch the boat back to England but found he had missed it by five minutes. Realising he had no option but to stay in Dublin for the night, Mr Vincent took a stroll around the city. His attention was attracted by the names over a theatre: 'Dwight L Moody and Ira D Sankey'. Wondering if it might be some Vaudeville Company, he decided to go in. The place was heaving with people and, as he entered the theatre, Mr Vincent was surprised to see people – in ordinary clothes – up on the platform. A man with an amazing voice was singing:

> *There were ninety and nine that safely lay,*
> *In the shelter of the fold,*
> *But one was out on the hills away,*
> *Far off from the gates of gold.*

The song mesmerised him and he then heard Moody speak.

3

Mr Vincent did not catch the boat the next day, or the next. Instead, he stayed on. Night after night he attended the meetings. Finally, one evening, he followed a great throng of people who rose from their seats to go to an Enquiry Room. None other than D L Moody knelt beside him and, after asking his name, simply asked, 'Do you believe Jesus Christ died for you?' When Mr Vincent replied that he did, Moody said 'Then, thank Him.'

He did and left that room a transformed man.[1]

Around the same time, Edward Studd purchased what he considered to be a superb racing horse. He entered the horse in an important race and wrote to many of his friends, including Mr Vincent, to tell them about his new purchase and the race the horse was running in. 'If you are a wise man, you will come to the race, and put every penny you can on my horse,'[2] wrote Edward.

He was too busy on the day of the races to see all his friends. However, when he next bumped into Mr Vincent, he asked him how much he had put on the horse. His friend replied, 'Not a penny'. Edward was indignant at this and told him he was a fool. Even so, he invited his friend to have dinner with him at his place at 2 Hyde Park Gardens. He told him he could decide afterwards where they would go to enjoy themselves for the evening.

When the meal was over, Mr Vincent suggested they visit the Drury Lane Theatre. Edward was surprised at this since he understood that this was where 'those fellows Moody and Sankey' were speaking. Instead, he suggested they go to a theatre or concert. However, Mr Vincent was adamant, replying, 'You are a man of your word, and you said you would go where I chose.'

By this time Moody and Sankey had moved from Dublin to London, and were holding nightly meetings at the Drury Lane Theatre. Edward had read about them in the newspapers, where they'd taken up plenty of columns. Lord Shaftesbury complained because Moody told stories that were 'bordering on the humorous, even to the extent of provoking a laugh,'[3] and the national newspapers described them as 'vulgar.' Others proposed that Moody was only here to sell his hymn books and that Sankey wanted to sell organs similar to the *'kist o' whistles.'*[4]

Edward did not protest too much at Mr Vincent's suggestion. He had been intrigued as to why the newspapers were printing so much about the two men and was happy to hear them himself.[5]

When they arrived at the theatre, however, all of the seats had gone. With his good connections, Mr Vincent managed to gain them entry and into seats very near the front, facing Moody. Edward had never been in an event like it in all his life. He was captivated. He was so impressed that he told Mr Vincent he was going to return and hear more. He kept his word and returned repeatedly. Eventually, the day came when he committed his life to Christ.

Once he had made his commitment, Edward was determined to live his new life in what he considered a proper 'Christian' way. For fifty-six years he had enjoyed life and pursued horses and pleasure. Now he wanted to know whether it was alright for him as a Christian to carry on enjoying the races, playing cards, shooting, hunting, going to the theatre and attending balls. He therefore managed to arrange a meeting with Moody and asked him outright.

Moody told him straight that, as racing meant betting and gambling, he couldn't see any way that he could carry on doing those things. As for the rest, the decision was his to make.

However, Edward wanted more specific advice, about such things as the theatre and playing cards. In the end Moody told him: 'Mr Studd, you have children and people you love; you are now a saved man yourself, and you want to get them saved … As soon as you have won a soul, you won't care about any of the other things.'[6]

Moody knew what he was talking about. Edward's life changed, as did his wife's since she also committed her life to Christ. Edward found that the things that had brought him pleasure all his life, no longer interested him. He started by making changes in Tedworth House, supervising the servants in re-arranging the furniture at Tedworth, packing chairs and benches into the marble-floored dance-hall so that local people could be invited to hear preachers whom Edward invited to his home.

He shocked relatives and staff by stopping attending race meetings. He sold or gave away all his horses, apart from one for each of his sons to use for hunting. The change in Edward was summed up rather well by his coachman who, when asked by a guest if his master had 'become religious or something', remarked: 'Well sir, we don't know much about that, but all I can say is that though there's the same skin, there's a new man inside.'[7]

Reaching out to the Boys

Edward immediately became concerned for the spiritual well-being of all his family and staff. Because his boys had been at boarding school since the age of seven, they were not fully aware of all the ways their father lived his life. Before going to boarding school, they assumed all little boys grew up strapped to a saddle, dressed in little red coats, and taught to guide their horses over big fences!

Knowing nothing of their father's conversion, three of his sons at Eton, Kynaston, George and Charles, were delighted one day to receive a letter from their father, saying he had arranged with the school, for them to have a day out, and to meet him in London. It was the middle of term. They arranged with their servant – yes, they had a servant attending to every need – that their best clothes would be ready for them to wear.

As they travelled by train to Paddington station, where they had arranged to meet their father, the boys speculated where he might take them for a meal. They tried to think what shows were on at the London theatres and which one they might be going to. Having greeted each of them, Edward led them out of the station to an awaiting carriage. However, they were shocked when he told them he was taking them to a special performance at the Drury Lane Theatre, to hear Dwight Moody and Ira Sankey.

As far as the boys were concerned, they were already part of a Christian family. They attended the Anglican Church regularly, putting on their best clothes on a Sunday to go to church and then putting them away for the rest of the week. If the boys were honest, they considered Sunday to be a bore and were glad when Monday came. 'Sundays and being in Church was a bit like having a bad toothache and having to go to the dentist,'[8] was Charles's description of Church at that time. Suffice to say, the boys were not impressed with their visit to the Drury Lane theatre.

An even bigger shock was waiting the boys when they returned home from Eton for their first school holiday after the theatre trip. They could not believe the changes that had been made to their home life. Following Christ, had changed their father dramatically, the boys could see, but they were not convinced his form of Christianity was for them. They began to resent the pressure that started to put on them to become 'real' Christians. Charles later commented that 'Everyone in the house had a dog's life of it until they were converted.'[9]

Their father would often come into their rooms, at the end of the day, and want to talk with them about Christ. His constant question was whether they wanted to accept Christ as their Saviour. To avoid his questions, they sometimes pretended they were already asleep.

However, Edward would not give up on them, or on all his friends and acquaintances. He became an out-and-out evangelist. Revival preachers were invited to the house to hold meetings. Edward would ride into the countryside, inviting local people to come to the house and listen to the speakers he had booked … and they came in their hundreds. The meetings attracted people from miles around. Edward was overjoyed when some of those who attended, accepted Christ. When home from school, his three boys were expected to attend the meetings, but nothing they heard touched them.

Moody and Sankey did visit Eton School whilst the three brothers were there. Well not exactly visit the school but land adjacent to it!

Two old Etonians, Quinton Hogg and John Graham MP, decided to erect a large tent on private land adjacent to the school for a 'Moody and Sankey' meeting. The Eton headmaster said he would not oppose any boys who wanted to attend it. As news that Eton boys might be subjected to 'revivalist drama' seeped out, letters appeared in *The Times* newspaper questioning the rightness of allowing it. The Marquis of Bath rose in the House of Lords to ask if the Provost, who was the Chairman of the Governing Body, and the Headmaster, had given permission for boys to attend and suggested 'Nothing can be more fateful to the discipline of the school.'[10]

On the day of the meeting the police declared they could not be responsible for security and Quinton Hogg and John Graham had no choice but to abandon the meeting in the large tent. They approached the Mayor of Windsor who agreed to lease them the Windsor Town Hall. However, when the police told the Mayor that Eton boys had procured a large quantity of eggs, the Mayor withdrew his permission. Thankfully one of the neighbours offered his large garden.

Later that afternoon, Moody stood on a chair under a chestnut tree as one hundred and fifty boys, four masters and two to three hundred parents quietly listened. Sankey sang. Moody preached. No records have been kept of which parents and boys attended. It can only be assumed that Edward Studd was one of the parents and Kynaston, Charles and George were among the boys.

Commitment Time

It was the long summer holiday break of 1877. The Studd boys thought they would play a prank on one of the preachers that their father had invited to speak at the Sunday meeting on the estate. His name was Mr Wetherby – 'Old Wetherby' they called him. The boys considered him a humourless man and a bit of a weakling. They knew he was not good at horse-riding and they quickly discovered he was not much good at cricket either. They therefore tricked him into coming on a ride with them and made sure it was scary, to say the least. Despite their best efforts, Wetherby managed to stay in his saddle, and so earned the grudging admiration of the boys. As they ended the ride, rather than being angry with them, he simply smiled and remarked that it was a 'nice day for a ride.'

That same afternoon Wetherby decided it was time to talk to the boys individually. He managed to speak with the boys privately and Kynaston, George and Charles each made a prayer of commitment to Christ. Charles was later to describe how it happened:

> Dashing out of the door arrayed in flannels to play cricket, he [Old Wetherby] caught me unawares and asked: 'Are you a Christian, young man?'
>
> I was taken aback and stuttered a reply: 'I am not what you call a Christian. I have believed on Jesus Christ since I was knee high, Sir. Of course, I believe in the Church, too.'
>
> I thought with such an answer I would get rid of him; but he persisted, quoting John 3:16.
>
> 'Do you believe Jesus Christ died?'
>
> 'Yes.'
>
> 'You believe He died for you?'
>
> 'Yes.'
>
> 'Do you believe the other half of the verse – 'shall have everlasting life'?'
>
> 'No,' I said. 'I don't believe that.'
>
> Old Wetherby responded: 'Now, don't you see that your statement contradicts God? Either God, or you, are not speaking the truth, for they contradict one another. Which is it? Do you think God is a liar?'
>
> 'No,' I said.
>
> 'Well, then, aren't you inconsistent, believing one half of the verse and not the other half?'
>
> 'I suppose I am.'
>
> 'Are you always going to be inconsistent?'

'No,' I said. 'Not always.'

'Will you be consistent now,' the speaker pressed?

I saw that I was cornered, and I began to think, If I go out of this room inconsistent, I won't carry very much self-respect. So I said: 'Yes, I will be consistent.'

'Well, don't you see that eternal life is a gift? When someone gives you a present, what do you do?'

'I take it and say, 'thank you.''

He said: 'Will you say 'thank you' to God for this gift?'

Then I got down on my knees and I did say 'thank you' to God. And right then and there, joy and peace came into my soul. I knew then what it was to be 'born again', and the Bible, which had been so dry to me before, became everything … well for at least a while! [11]

None of the boys knew about the encounters the others had had with Old Wetherby and the commitment they had each made to Christ. None of them wanted to tell anyone else what had happened – except their father. After they returned to Eton for the autumn term, Charles wrote and told his father what had happened to him. 'Dear Father, I should have told you …' the letter began. 'When Mr Wetherby came, I invited Christ into my life…'[12]

To his amazement a letter addressed to all three brothers arrived one morning at Eton from their father. It told them the news that all three had made a commitment to Christ on the same day! As they talked, they shared how they had been reading the Bible and praying every day since then. They decided to start a Bible Study group at Eton with some of their close friends – some of whom went on to have strong Christian influences in later life.

Father's Death

By 1879, Charles's brothers, Kynaston and George had left Eton. Life was good for Charles, or CT as all his friends referred to him. He was captain of the Eton First Eleven cricket team and represented Eton at racquets.

But in the November, he received a summons to leave a Latin lesson and go to the Headmaster's study. CT wondered what he could have done wrong. It was not often he was summoned in such a way.

He could never have imagined the news he was about to hear. His father was dead. CT was devastated. How could such a thing be possible? The last time he had seen him, he had been so fit and well. A carriage was immediately called to take CT home, to be with the family.

Once home, he heard the news of what had happened. His father and mother had left Tedworth House to travel to one of Moody's meetings. On the way Edward suddenly remembered he had forgotten to bring with him one of the grooms, who he wanted to hear the gospel. He stopped the carriage.

Because they were already late for the meeting, he told his coachman to take the others on to the meeting, telling him he would find the groom and the two of them would ride along together. He jumped out and ran all the way back to the house to tell the groom to come. However, on the way back, a blood vessel in his leg burst.

On her return home later that evening, Dora found her husband lying on the couch. She called the doctor but nothing could be done. Edward never recovered and by the next morning he was dead.

At his funeral the clergyman who led the service told the congregation that Edward Studd had done 'more in two years as a Christian than most Christians do in twenty,'[13] through the fearless way he had shared the gospel with anyone he met. To those he could not speak to, he wrote letters – often receiving terse replies in return!

Thankfully Edward had put his affairs in order. He had made a Will setting out everything that was to happen to all his possessions. The Will handed the family estate to Kynaston as the eldest son, with the proviso that his wife could remain in residence in the Hyde Park house until her death. To each of his sons a large sum of money was left, which they would inherit on their twenty-fifth birthday.

CHAPTER 2

Cricket Superstar

It may surprise some readers to know that football was not always the dominant sport of the nation. Although it was played in the 1880s, it was not in the manner of today. The FA Cup only began in 1871 and the first ever football league was still to come in 1888. Horse racing was much more popular, as was a form of racquet playing. But the most popular sport was cricket. In terms of personalities who represented the best of cricket, the Studd brothers, and in particular CT, were at the very top. They were the superstars of their day.

In later life CT was to say that he never regretted playing cricket, though he regretted that he had allowed it to become an idol. However, he knew that the qualities he had learned on the cricket field – of courage, self-denial and endurance – were the qualities that he applied to his life once he was fully consecrated to the Lord.

For the three brothers, apart from their academic studies, cricket was their life. All three were members of the Eton School cricket XI at the same time; the first time such a thing had happened at Eton. It was 1877, the year of their father's conversion. Kynaston was nineteen and captain. The next brother was eighteen-year old George and then came Charles, seventeen.

In one of the games against Winchester – which Eton won by an innings – their scores in the first innings were Kynaston 52 runs, Charles 53 and George 54. Reports of the matches were full of praise for the brothers, with one predicting that 'Charles Studd … should make a great name someday.'[1] Another report for 1879 placed CT alongside C F H Leslie, the Rugby Captain, as the best all-round Public School player of that year.[2]

As CT left Eton, his housemaster, Mr Cameron, wrote of him:

> Perhaps he might have done more in work, but it is hard
> for the Captain of the XI and he had done no little good to
> all who have come under his influence. I think the secret
> of the charm of his character is that he thinks for others
> rather than himself. We shall miss him terribly and it is
> sad parting.[3]

Because of CT's ability as a cricketer at Eton, he was given his Cricket Blue immediately he went up to Trinity College, Cambridge, in the autumn of 1879. That was a very unusual achievement for a freshman. He was to remain in the team for four years and was captain for one of those years.

It was never really known if CT's ability with the bat was down to genius, or hard work. Some say CT's skills as a cricketer were mainly down to his thoroughness of preparation. When he set his mind to do something, he was single-minded in his efforts. CT developed his cricket skill by standing in front of a big wardrobe mirror. It had a carpet in front with a seam running down the centre. Here he practised a 'straight bat' for hours on end. *Lillywhite's Cricket Record* for the year said of CT:

> Very few players have a finer style: brilliant leg hitting and
> driving, with a very hard wrist stroke in front of point;
> a real straight bat, and a resolute nerve make together a
> batsman whose back bowlers are very glad to see.

Such was CT's desire to be the best 'batter' that he had an intense dislike of smoking. As a batsman, he considered his eyes were key in being able to identify the length of pitch the bowler would bowl. It was the custom in those days to 'light-up' after dinner was finished. That was always CT's cue to leave the dining room, lest the smoke affect his eyes.

By 1882, he was at the height of his game. Still at Cambridge, he rose to the very top of the cricket world, amateur and professional alike, becoming only the second Englishman to achieve the 'double' of 1,000 runs and 100 wickets in a season.[4] He did in fact score 1,249 runs and captured a total of 131 wickets in the 1882 season.

Lillywhite's Cricket Record for that year said:

> Mr C T Studd must be given premier position among
> the batsmen of 1882 and it would be difficult to instance
> a finer innings by so young a cricketer against the best
> bowling of the day than his three-figure scores against
> Australia and the Players. One of the classiest batsmen
> of his era, by far the best bowler among the Gentlemen
> cricketers, and an excellent fielder … at the tender age of
> twenty-two he was the toast of English cricket.'[5]

In the three matches *Lillywhite's Cricket Record* was referring to, CT made 118 playing against Australia, 100 for the Gentlemen v Players at Lord's and 126 not out when playing against The Gentlemen of England.

In 1882, CT was transformed from being considered the best cricketer by his peers, to becoming the most famous household name in England – well, at least among those who were interested in sport.

Monday 29 May 1882 was a warm sunny day and there was a nervousness around the Fenner's cricket ground in Cambridge. The mighty Australian cricket team were coming to play a University of Cambridge eleven in a three-day match. Mighty because, in the ten weeks they had been touring England, they had been victorious in every game they had played.

The newspapers of the day talked about the strongest Australian cricket team that had ever been seen. They had scored 206 runs against Oxford University and, at the Hove cricket ground, had thrashed Sussex by a massive innings and 355 runs. Their visit to the Kennington Oval had seen them pull off a stunning victory against Surrey. The team included such famous players as Murdoch, Massie, Bowle and the demon bowler Spoffirth, whom some thought was the greatest bowler there had ever been.

Charles Studd's brother, George, was captain of Cambridge Cricket that year. When he had been asked if Cambridge would play a game against Australia during the summer term, he had readily agreed. However, many, including the President of the Cambridge Cricket Club, thought that the University team would be soundly beaten and disgrace themselves. But they had not considered the impact of the Studd brothers, especially CT.

On the first day of the match interest in the Australia team was immense and the crowds who came to watch were said to be the largest ever recorded. Australia were a strong team and everyone – well almost everyone – expected an Australian victory. However, *Punch* magazine nicknamed the Studd brothers (Kynaston, Charles and George) the 'set of Studds', a point noted before the match by Tom Horan, a left-arm blower in the Australia team: 'I hear they [Cambridge] have a set of Studds in the eleven. We shall win as long as we can get them out.' He was right. They didn't get them out and didn't win!

A banker had three gold studs made for his evening dress shirt. Each stud had a different brother's initials on them. Whoever scored the most runs on any day, where all three were playing, went to the top of his shirt that night.[6]

Australia won the toss and their openers, Bannerman and Massie, walked out to the crease. The crowd gave them a lively welcome. Australia made a good start to their first innings. Initially, against the bowling of C T Studd and Ramsay, runs came easily for Australia. However, a quick and surprising collapse meant the entire side was out for 139. CT took five wickets for 64 runs and Ramsay also took five wickets.

Kynaston and George Studd were the openers for Cambridge. Kynaston was soon out and then Cambridge went three wickets down for only 55 runs. That's when CT, aged just 21, joined his brother at the crease. A remarkable innings began.

Unfortunately, when Cambridge had reached 89 runs, George was clean bowled by Spofforth for 42 – 'an innings of part brilliance and part chance.'[7]

William Bather now became CT's partner and together they resisted the Australian bowling and made a good run score. There was much cheering when they reached a 100, and then CT made a splendid on-drive for four. The ball almost pitched into the spectators. The runs were piling on rapidly. There was a roar of applause when the Australian total was passed. The Australian's captain, Murdoch, kept changing the bowlers, but it made no difference. At the end of the day's play, CT was not out at 85 and Bather 20. The score was 187 for four wickets. As they came off the field, they received a rousing reception.

Play was resumed on the Tuesday. More people wanted to attend, sensing something special was happening in the match. Special trains were put on to bring the crowds. The pessimism of the first day had been replaced by an expectation of success.

> Bather was soon bowled, and Ralph Spencer, then Percival Henry, joined CT. CT completed his 100 amidst great cheering. He added two more fours and a single before being caught. He walked back to a great ovation having scored a magnificent 118. The side were eventually out for 266.[8]

In the second innings the Australians achieved 290, leaving Cambridge to make 168 to win. Opinion was divided as to whether they could do it a second time.

Kynaston and George were first in. Cheer greeted every run as they raced up to a partnership of 106 runs. It all looked too easy. Then there was a mini collapse by Cambridge but, eventually, the winning run was struck by CT who was not out with 17 runs. Cambridge had beaten Australia by six wickets.

The match was the making of the Studd brothers and especially CT. His name was on everyone's lips. Before the season was finished, he had made another century against Australia. In the entire season only three centuries were scored against Australia and CT got two of them. His face became instantly recognisable and everywhere he went, he was asked for his autograph.

Later in the year, Australia beat England in a match at the Kennington Oval (Surrey cricket ground) in South London. It was on 28 August 1882 and out of it the Ashes came into existence – today considered the most important contest in cricket.

A record crowd of over 20,000 gathered on a rather cold day at the Oval to watch the match. CT was part of the England team. Apart from CT, the English XI consisted of the legendary W G Grace (a doctor who served the poor in Bristol),[9] R G Barlow, G Ulyett, A P Lucas, A Lyttelton, J M Read, W Barnes, A G Steel, A N Hornby (Captain) and E Peate.

For some reason the Captain, 'Monkey' Hornby, decided to alter the batting order. CT went in eighth, with just eight runs needed for England to win. With him at the crease two other wickets fell. He never received a single ball. England lost. The loss was seen as a great humiliation to the English team. It was the first time they had lost a test series to a team from the 'colonies'.

A few days after the match *The Sporting Times* newspaper published the following mock obituary to English cricket:

In affectionate remembrance

OF

ENGLISH CRICKET,

WHICH DIED AT THE OVAL

ON

29 AUGUST 1882

Deeply lamented by a large circle of sorrowing
friends and acquaintances.

RIP

---

*NB The body will be cremated and the
ashes taken to Australia.*

The following winter, 1882, whilst Kynaston was organising a Moody and Sankey mission at Cambridge University, CT and George were invited to be part of the English test team to tour Australia and Ceylon. The team was under the captaincy of Hon Ivo Bligh, (later to become Lord Darney) and a lifelong friend of CT.

Punch magazine said they were going on a quest to recover the Ashes!

England lost the first test at Melbourne cricket ground but they went on to win the next at Melbourne and then the final test at Sydney cricket ground on the 17 February 1883.

It was after the third test, and as the England team were preparing to return home, that a group of Melbourne ladies were introduced to them. The ladies produced a small silver urn which they said contained the ashes from a burnt cricket bail. They gave it to Ivo Bligh. On the urn were inscribed the words:

When Ivo goes back with the urn, the urn
Studds, Steel, Read and Tylecote return, return!

The welkin will ring loud,
The great crowd will feel proud
Seeing Barlow and Bates with the urn, the urn
And the rest coming home with the urn.

The history of the Ashes had begun!

One of the newspaper reporters covering the tour, was present to capture the scene. He telegraphed a report back to England. When the players' ship docked in London, a crowd had gathered, eager to see the Ashes. The urn, with the ash still inside it and the writing on the side, is now a famous exhibit in the Lord's Cricket Ground museum.

By now a recognisable face and a name familiar to most people, CT returned to captain Cambridge in his last year, 1883. For the second year running he was declared the best all-round cricketer in Britain, having scored 1,193 runs at 41.13 – a great average at that time – and captured 112 wickets at 17.47 with nine five-wicket hauls.

The *Cricketing Annual* recorded:

> Mr C T Studd must for the second year in succession be
> accorded the premier position as an all-round cricketer.
> Some years have elapsed since the post has been filled by
> a player so excellent in all three departments of the game.
> His batting especially has been of the highest class.

The famous cricketer, W G Grace, called him: 'the most brilliant member of a well-known cricketing family [who] from 1881-84 had few superiors as an all-round player.'[10]

Despite his cricketing commitment and glory, he completed his BA degree and came down from Cambridge in 1884. He went on to join Middlesex.[11] A great cricketing career looked to be stretching in front of him. But, as CT rose to prominence in the cricket world, and especially while touring with the test team in Australia, there were a number of family and friends who were praying for him that he would rediscover the Lord he had committed his life to as a boy.

The only brother who was outstanding in his witness for the Lord Jesus Christ during those cricketing years was Kynaston. Years later Charles wrote to him from Africa and said:

> I have never forgotten the influence your life has been on me, and how I admired your courage and loyalty to the Lord Jesus Christ, which earned for you the greatest of all compliments. Remember our cricketing friends used to call you 'The Austere Man', because your life was true to God and you were true to them; for you were ever faithful speaking to them about their souls.'

CHAPTER 3

Cambridge and Recommitment

Moody and Sankey at Cambridge

The University of Cambridge is the second oldest university in the English speaking world, with some of its colleges dating back to the fourteenth and fifteenth centuries. The oldest college, Peterhouse, dates back to 1284, and Trinity College, where the Studd brothers studied and considered one of the most prestigious of colleges, was founded by Henry VIII in 1546.

In the nineteenth century most of the traditions of the University were as archaic as the colleges themselves. In 1882, no undergraduate would dream of walking out without wearing a hat and a walking stick in hand. Gradually reform was coming. There had been a Statutory Commission set up in 1877 to consider changes at the University, but change was slow! From 1882, dons for the first time were allowed to marry. Girton and Newhaven

Colleges had opened for women, and were gradually being accepted as part of the University. Even so, with the exception of those two colleges, Cambridge was very much a 'men's only' university.

In 1882 George was captain of the Cambridge cricket team and Kynaston was President of the Cambridge Inter-Collegiate Christian Union. As President, Kynaston proposed that the American evangelists, Moody and Sankey, be invited to Cambridge for a series of meetings, the following Michaelmas (autumn) term. However, there was much resistance within the student body – the majority of the staid Cambridge University students did not like the idea.

Back in 1875 Moody and Sankey had held their Great London Campaign. Early evening meetings were held in the East End of London for 'the poor of the docks and the slums.'[1] Then they would travel across to Her Majesty's Opera House, in Haymarket, where the rich and famous arrived in their carriages. The Princess of Wales told an evangelical peer what a help Moody had been to her. It is said that Lord Chancellor Cairns, and even William Gladstone and Matthew Arnold, sat at the feet of this unlettered man. People had to acknowledge that wherever the two men had travelled throughout the British Isles, they had drawn immense crowds as Moody preached and Sankey sang.

The Cambridge University students and dons debated the proposal. Kynaston was persuasive; he knew the effect Moody had had on his own father. Eventually it was agreed that Moody and Sankey could come and would hold meetings – in the town in the afternoon, and for the undergraduates in the evening.

Unfortunately the timing of the visit meant CT and his brother George played no part in the meetings. They had previously been chosen to be part of the England cricket team to tour Australia throughout the Michaelmas term.

As the term began, posters were plastered all over the University and the town. Kynaston signed a personal invitation to every one of the 3,500 undergraduates attending that year.[2]

The meetings began on Sunday 5 November, Bonfire Night – the day that T R Glover described as: 'a night consecrated to disorder, to bonfires and fireworks, and to fights between town and gown.'[3]

The town meeting in the afternoon went well. However, the meeting in the evening at the University was a disaster, even though 1,700 attended. The University audience sang rowdy songs; they built a pyramid of chairs in the middle of the auditorium; a fire cracker was thrown against a window. Disturbances continued throughout the evening, with bursts of laughter, loud talking and shouts of 'Well done'.

The second night was not much better with only about hundred undergraduates present. Even so, five of those at the meeting committed their lives to Christ.

It was on the Wednesday night that something broke. After the afternoon town meeting, Moody asked mothers in the audience to stay behind and pray for the undergraduates. Two hundred did. The atmosphere at the University meeting that evening was different. For the first time Moody invited a public response. At first no one moved. Then one student responded, and another and another. In all fifty-two men made the walk.

On the Thursday night Sankey sang the hymn 'There were ninety and nine'. Then Moody spoke on sowing and reaping. The following evening, a hundred students responded to the call to commit their lives to Christ.

The climax came on the Sunday evening, 12 November. Four meetings were held in all that day. Nearly two thousand university men were present for the final meeting. There was no opposition or interruptions. Moody preached on the text: 'The angel said to them, fear not for I bring you good news' (Luke 2:10).

After the choir sang the hymn, 'Just as I am without one plea', Moody led in prayer and then asked those who had been blessed during the week to stand. At least 200 rose to their feet. Included in that number were Trinity undergraduates, Arthur Polhill-Turner and Dixon Hoste, who later became part of the Cambridge Seven.

The Moody and Sankey meetings were to have a profound effect on the entire University. The Vice-Principal of Ridley Hall College commented, 'I think there is not one man here whose life was not influenced … by Moody's Cambridge Mission.'[4]

Although it was not the intention of the Moody and Sankey meetings, many of those who responded at their meetings felt the call to mission. It paved the way for what was to happen a few years later when the Cambridge Seven held their own meetings at the University.

At George's Bedside

Having graduated from Cambridge, CT assumed that he would enjoy life and his fame as part of the English cricket team before settling down as an English country squire with a successful secular career. However, in early 1884 news reached CT that his brother George was seriously ill with pneumonia. He found it hard to believe because only a few months earlier the two of them had been fit and healthy in Australia.

As soon as CT heard the news, he rushed to George's bedside at their London home at 2 Hyde Park Gardens. Here CT found his brother looking 'horribly white and, as he breathed, his chest made horrible rattling noises'.[5] His doctor said there was nothing that could be done. All the family could do was pray for a miracle that he recover.

As CT kept a vigil at his bedside, and watched his brother hover between life and death, it caused him to question what life was all about. He had the fame and the fortune, but knew there had to be more to life. For George, the fragility of his own body, had already caused him to re-commit his life to the Lord Jesus Christ.

Sitting in a chair by George's bed, night after night, CT had plenty of time to think. He began to ask himself: 'Now what is all the world's popularity worth to George? ... What is fame and flattery worth? ... Is it worth possessing all the world's riches, when a man faces eternity?'[6] An inner voice seemed to whisper to him: 'Vanity of vanities, all is vanity' (Ecclesiastes 1:2).

As he sat watching his brother, not knowing if he would live or die, it dawned on him that cricket would never help anyone with the issues of life and death. He concluded that he had to do something that would help people with eternal values. It was on one of those nights, in early January 1884, that that he recommitted his life to Christ.

'God brought me back,'[7] was how CT described it. God also brought George through, for there came a day when he opened his eyes and grunted. His recovery had started.

Recommitment and Change

By the beginning of 1884 Moody and Sankey were back in the United Kingdom on the second stage of their gospel campaign. This time they were based in St Pancras, London, where temporary halls were erected at eleven different sites to allow as many people as possible, especially the poor, to hear the good news.

When CT was sure that George was well enough for him to be able to leave him, he went again and listened to Moody speak. It was there that the Lord met him afresh. He restored to him 'the joy of (his) salvation' (Psalm 51:12).

His life changed and he began to re-evaluate what he was doing. In particular, CT was challenged through reading a tract which a friend gave him in which an atheist had written:

> If I were a thoroughly consistent Christian man, my whole life would be given up in going about the world preaching the gospel. I should consider the pleasures, the honours, and the riches of this world as dross. I should count the sorrows and pains of this world as nothing.
>
> My whole life would be spent in pleading with men to be reconciled to God through the Lord Jesus Christ and warning them what they must suffer if they still persisted in rejecting Him.
>
> I would be restless in season and out of season. I would not care what the world thought or did. As I went about, my text would be, 'what shall it profit a man if he gain the whole world and lose his own soul'.[8]

When he had prayed with Old Wetherby all those years ago as a schoolboy, home from Eton for a few weeks, CT had been ashamed to reveal to people what he had done. This time there was no holding him back; he was immediately challenged to start witnessing about his faith.

The majority of CT's friends and acquaintances were students and into sport. He therefore started meeting up with a group of athletes for Bible Study and prayer. They began to plan how they could reach out to other athletes and students on the campus.

CT also began helping his brother Kynaston organise missions amongst the students. He loved witnessing and was fearless in speaking with other undergraduates about Christ. The two of them were invited to speak at some of the fringe meetings of the Moody campaigns. Their words impacted many young people who came to listen to them, initially because of their fame as cricketers.

An example of one person whose life was turned around, was a young student doctor by the name of William Grenfell. He was returning to his digs one evening, having seen a patient, when he saw a large tent, filled with people. He went to see what was going on and found out that it was part of the Moody and Sankey campaign. In his autobiography Grenfell later wrote:

> I went down to hear the brothers Kynaston and Charles
> Studd speak at some subsidiary meeting of the Moody
> campaign. They were natural athletes, and I felt that I
> could listen to them … Never shall I forget, after the
> Studd brothers had spoken, the audience being asked
> to stand up if they intended to try to follow Christ. It
> appeared a very sensible question to me, but I was amazed
> how hard I found it to stand up. At last one boy, out of
> a hundred or more in sailor rig, from an industrial or
> reformatory ship on the Thames, suddenly rose. It seemed
> to me such a wonderfully courageous act – for I knew
> perfectly what it would mean to him – that I immediately
> found myself on my feet, and went out feeling that I had
> crossed the Rubicon, and must do something to prove it.[9]

As the cricket season progressed, CT shared his faith with those who were members of his team. At his encouragement, many of the England cricket XI went to hear Moody preach, amongst them A G Steel and the captain of the test team, Ivo Bligh. Bligh wrote to CT after attending one of the meetings and said: 'An address from that man (DL Moody) goes right home and makes one think more than any man I have heard.'[10]

There had been a time when CT had thought his life would be cricket, cricket and more cricket. Now CT knew that cricket could no longer be the basis of his life. There had to be more to it. However, despite three months of reading the Bible, praying and asking friends for advice, he had no specific guidance. He was becoming quite anxious for an answer. All around him, as the summer term of 1884 progressed, his friends knew what they were going to do. He decided that, until the Lord showed him differently, he would study law. However, as soon as he made this decision, he began having doubts.

CT's inheritance from his father was more than sufficient to live on for the rest of his life. However, he began to wonder how he could spend the best years of his life working for himself and for the honour and pleasures of this world, whilst thousands and thousands of souls were perishing every day without having heard of the Lord Jesus Christ?

The Lord was working. CT was living a consistent Christian life but not experiencing the peace and the joy that the Lord promised in his Word. During this time, CT came across a book which in time was to become a best-seller across the UK. It was titled: *The Christian's Secret of a Happy Life* by Hannah Whitall Smith[11]. It talked about the blessing God extended to everyone who was ready and willing to receive it. The book showed how the Bible taught that Christians could live lives of rest and triumph. To do so, Hannah Whitall Smith wrote, there were two steps they had to follow – first, entire abandonment and, second, absolute faith.[12]

CT realised that he had not received that blessed rest as he had not fully yielded his life to the Lord. Although he had known about Jesus Christ's dying for him, he 'had never understood that if he died for me, then I didn't belong to myself.' He came to realise he 'had been keeping back from God what belonged to Him.'[13] So, he fell on his knees in his room and yielded himself afresh to the Lord, using the words of Frances Ridley Havergal's consecration hymn.

Take my life and let it be
Consecrated Lord to Thee;
Take my moments and my days,
Let them flow in ceaseless praise.

From that time on, his life became one of simple, childlike faith. He came to understand that his part was to trust and allow the Lord to do His good pleasure in him. All the anxiety of the last few months left him. In its place came peace and joy.

The Pull of England

CT had always assumed that England was to be his mission field. How the country needed to hear the gospel message! Though most of the population still attended church and the country could boast of great preachers such as Charles Spurgeon and Bishop Ryle, the Christianity most people experienced was a mere shadow of the real thing. CT understood Paul's words in 2 Timothy 3.5: 'Having a form of godliness, but denying the power thereof: from such turn away.'

CT was not yet aware of the homelessness, poverty and terrible working conditions that existed underneath the veneer of Queen Victoria's respectable Britain. He knew of William Booth and the work his Salvation Army was doing. He had heard the stories of the terrible persecution he and his followers were experiencing simply because they had shared Christ with those the Church was failing to reach.

However, new and challenging teachings were emerging in society. Charles Darwin was beginning to expound his theories and shake many people's faith. German theologians were declaring the Bible was not really a special book containing God's infallible word. Their teaching was spreading rapidly in British colleges and universities.

How Britain needed strong Christian leaders of the quality of C T Studd. Was that his calling? Was his role to counter these false teachings? These were the questions that CT started asking.

CHAPTER 4

Onward Christian Soldiers

G od was about to do something amazing in the British Isles. However, this would not be for the direct benefit of the Church in Britain itself, but for people overseas, especially those in China. Very soon there were so many young Christians wanting to fulfil the Lord's commission to 'go and make disciples of all nations' (Matthew 28:18) that Church leaders were reminding those who came to talk to them not to forget the British Isles. Perhaps the Lord was wanting them to serve there rather than overseas?

The reason for this impact on the nation was a group of men who came to be known as the Cambridge Seven. One of the seven was C T Studd.

China Calling

The first Englishman to serve as a missionary in China was Robert Morrison, who arrived in China in 1807. By 1865, thirty different Protestant groups were working there, including the London Missionary Society, the American Board of Commissioners for Foreign Missions, and many missionaries attached to their denominations, eg Baptists, Southern Baptists, Presbyterians, American Reformed Mission, Methodists, Episcopalians and Wesleyans.

However, in the seven provinces in which Protestant missionaries were working, there were an estimated 204 million people and only 91 workers. Eleven other provinces with a population estimated at 197 million, had no Protestant Christian witness.

Being a missionary in China was tough! If their primary objective was the conversion of the Chinese to Christianity, they had little success. The first Protestant missionary, Robert Morrison, in 27 years of missionary effort, only knew of twenty-five converts. Other missionaries had similar experiences. The pace of conversions picked up with time but, by the beginning of the twentieth century there were still only an estimated 100,000 Chinese Protestant Christians, after nearly a century of endeavour by thousands of missionaries. Many of those converted were considered 'rice Christians' – who accepted Christianity only for the material benefits that were attached to becoming a Christian. In the end missionaries turned towards establishing hospitals and schools as a more effective way in attracting the Chinese towards Christianity.

China Inland Mission

However, one missionary who had a powerful and long-lasting effect on the evangelising of China was James Hudson Taylor, who set up the China Inland Mission (now OMF International).

Hudson Taylor was born into a loving Christian family, in England in 1832. His father was a preacher who was fascinated by China.

However, during his teenage years, Hudson Taylor turned his back on Christianity, living for himself and scoffing at religion. One day, as he browsed through the books in his father's study, he selected one, not realising its Christian content. At that very time his mother, some 75 miles away, was praying for his salvation. That day her prayers were answered in the most dramatic way as Hudson Taylor committed his life to Christ. His life changed immediately and he felt God's call to China.

For four years he studied, preached, and trained in medicine, before sailing to China as the first missionary with the Chinese Evangelization Society. He was only 21 years of age.

When Hudson Taylor arrived in China, the country was in the middle of civil war and there was an intense hatred of foreigners. Angry mobs threatened his life many times, he was robbed of everything and the mission he went to China with ran out of money. However, he persevered in the work and met and married his wife, Maria Dyer.

Returning to England in 1860, Hudson Taylor sensed God's call to birth a new kind of mission work that reached the people of inland China. The China Inland Mission was born. His prayer was that God would raise up twenty-four missionaries and the finances to make the journey back to China. Volunteers were welcomed from all walks of life, single or married, men or women, educated or not.

Within a year Hudson Taylor saw God provide all of that and more. His slogan for funding was: 'God's work, done in God's way, will never lack God's supply.'

By the age of fifty-two, Hudson Taylor had become a legend in missionary circles. Despite having buried a wife and five of her nine children; suffered numerous illnesses; and had many injuries from attacks by the Chinese people, he had lost none of his zeal and passion for the lost.[1]

Hudson Taylor saw the China Inland Mission as a new and very different kind of mission, based on the principles of faith and prayer. He set as his goal to reach the interior of China where none of the other missionary organisations had dared to venture.

In the early 1880s (when CT was at Cambridge), the China Inland Mission was little known in Britain. That was about to change dramatically. Some of Hudson Taylor's writings had begun to circulate, and those who read them were impressed.

Dixon Hoste (one of the Cambridge Seven) wrote: 'I became deeply impressed by the single-heartedness, self-denying devotion to the cause of the gospel in China which characterised the writings of Mr Hudson Taylor and others.'[2] He read in Hudson Taylor's booklet, *China's Spiritual Need and Claims*, of the 385 million in China 'utterly and hopelessly beyond the reach of the gospel' and Hudson Taylor's challenge:

'Can the Christians of England sit still with folded arms while these multitudes are perishing?'[3]

Hudson Taylor knew his role was to lead the work in China, but he also knew that he needed to spend time in the UK sharing his vision and challenging Christians to serve. As Christians met this fifty-one-year-old missionary, they could not help but be impressed by 'his kindliness of manner, his unobtrusive humour, his steel hardened will, tempered by the indefinable redolence of Christ's presence.'[4]

One of the early recruits to the China Inland Mission was thirty-one-year-old Dr Harold Schofield who was educated at Oxford University and had become a brilliant young doctor in the UK. In 1880 Dr Schofield responded to the call of God, becoming a missionary doctor with the China Inland Mission.

In time he became the first Protestant missionary allowed to go into the interior of China, to a place called Taiyuan, the capital of the province of Shansi in northern China – a teeming mass of nine million inhabitants, some four hundred miles inland. Dr Schofield could think of only another five or six missionaries at work in the entire region.

When he was not out dispensing medicines, and caring for the sick and needy who came to the little surgery attached to his house, he spent time in his prayer closet. His burden was very specific – to pray that God would send more labourers into his vineyard, particularly labourers who had the ability to lead. He prayed for many more 'men of culture, education, and distinguished gifts, intellectual as well as spiritual' to come to the mission field.[5]

Dr Schofield knew God could use anyone but, as he laboured amongst the Chinese people, he specifically identified the need for God to raise up men who were trained for leadership. His heart prayer was that God would touch the universities of the United Kingdom and call from them men of talent and ability consecrating them for His work in China. It seemed an impossible prayer since Dr Schofield knew that when he had left England some two and half years previously, there were very few in the universities who were interested in mission, and even fewer responding to the call of mission in China.

By 1883, at the age of only thirty-two, Harold Schofield lay dying in his house in Taiyuan. He had caught diphtheria from one of his Chinese patients and the strain was untreatable. However, he kept praying to the end that God would stir the hearts of British university graduates to the needs of China. When he died on 1 August 1883, his last words were a request to 'tell Mr Taylor and the Council ... that these three years in China have been by far the happiest of my life.'[6]

Harold Schofield never knew during all the time that he prayed that God had heard his cry and was going to answer it in a dramatic way. Just a few days after his death, the first of those who became known as the Cambridge Seven had their interview with Hudson Taylor about going to China.[7]

The Cambridge Seven

So who were they, this small band of elite academics and sports men from the top university of the day? Before we look at the seven individuals, let's remind ourselves of something we read in the Scriptures.

In his letter to the Corinthian church, the apostle Paul wrote:

Not many wise ... not many mighty, not many noble are
called. But God has chosen the foolish things of the world
to put to shame the wise, and God has chosen the weak
things of the world to put to shame the things that are
mighty, and the base things of the world and the things
which are despised God has chosen, and the things which

are not, to bring to nothing the things that are, that no
flesh should glory in His presence.[8]

That certainly does not sound like the Cambridge Seven, who came
from the cream of society, and all with aristocratic upbringings.
They had parents and relatives of wealth, status and important
positions in society. They were educated at the finest schools in
the country and went to the top universities of their day. Two of
them were officers in Her Majesty's Army. 'The influence of such a
band of men going forth to China as missionaries was irresistible,'
wrote Dr Eugene Stock, of the Church Missionary Society. 'No
such event had occurred before,' he added, 'and no event of the
century did so much to arouse the minds of Christian men to
the tremendous claims of the Field, and the nobility of the
missionary vocation.'[9]

Undoubtedly, in the British public's eye, the star of the
Cambridge Seven was C T Studd, but there were seven men in
total. Who were the other six who made up the Cambridge Seven?

Stanley Smith

Stanley P Smith had parents who loved the Lord. As a thirteen-
year-old, in 1874, he had been taken to hear Moody speaking in
Eastbourne and committed his life to the Saviour. His desire at the
time was to become a Church of England minister.

However, five years later his faith had grown cold. Boating,
bathing, rowing, playing the new and exciting game of lawn tennis
and cycling his penny-farthing with the 52-inch wheel filled his
life. Even with all this activity his health was not good and he
suffered with colds, chills and a sore chest.

When he arrived at Cambridge in the October of 1879, Stanley joined the rowing club and teamed up with friends from his old school, Repton – William Cassels and Montagu Beauchamp. It was during his second term that a second-year student, the Honourable Granville Waldegrave, came to visit him. Waldegrave had made it his mission to pray for Stanley. As they talked, Stanley had to admit he was only a luke-warm Christian.

From then on, every time they met, Waldegrave talked with Stanley about the Lord and one day challenged him to make a decision – it had to be all or nothing. Soon after Stanley made the decision to live by and for Christ.

When term finished at the end of his first year, Stanley used the long summer vacation to help at a mission hall in the East End of London with their work amongst the slums. This the first time Stanley had prayed extempore in public and then preached in the open air. After that he went on to Aldershot and helped at Miss Daniell's Soldiers' Home where 'the wonder of bringing soldiers to Christ "filled the cup of his joy".'[10]

Stanley didn't want to waste more time on education, but wanted to go straight to the mission field, so he wrote to his parents with his plans. Whilst not refusing, they told Stanley to be cautious and promised to pray for guidance. A chastened and more humble Stanley returned to Cambridge for his second year. His faith continued to grow and on the river his rowing blossomed. When he won the Maghaghten Sculls, he used his prize money to buy a copy of Holman Hunt's picture *The Light of the World*.

The Michaelmas term of 1881 saw Stanley captain the First Trinity Boat Club. When he was chosen as stroke of the Cambridge Varsity boat, he determined to speak with every man in the boat about Christ. He was known throughout Cambridge as a Christian.

With his degree gained in June 1882 Stanley saw ordination ahead of him. He began to be invited to speak at conferences and evangelistic events. However, on 30 November 1883 he believed the Lord indicated that He didn't want him to serve at home, but on the foreign mission field. Isaiah 49:6 was the verse God used to speak to him: 'I will also give you as a light to the Gentiles that you should be my salvation to the ends of the earth.'

Stanley had long had an interest in the work of the China Inland Mission. Before the end of the year, he therefore wrote to the CIM to tell them of his interest in serving with them. At the beginning of the following year, on 14 January, he met Hudson Taylor for a long talk about China, and this was followed, two months later, by a visit from Hudson Taylor to discuss things further and meet Stanley's parents.

Six days later, on 1 April, Stanley was interviewed at a CIM Council meeting and accepted as a probationer.

Stanley Smith remained in China until his death in 1931. Towards the end of his life there were theological differences between him and the CIM and he was forced to resign from the mission.

Montagu (Monty) Proctor-Beauchamp

Montagu (Monty) Proctor-Beauchamp was the fourth son of a baronet, which meant his father was called 'Sir Thomas'. He was a tall likeable lad who had occasional tempers. Within the family, Christ was spoken of openly and they were friends with Hudson Taylor. In fact, one of Monty's earliest memories was, as a boy of five, being regaled with stories about China, chopsticks and pigtails on one of Hudson Taylor's visits. The family had been one of the original sponsors of the China Inland Mission.

The Beauchamp family were good friends with the Studd family, as well as Stanley Smith (who was at Repton with Monty). Once they were all at Cambridge, CT's brother, Kynaston, in February 1881 asked Stanley to join him in praying for Monty on a daily basis. This he did and Kynaston was subsequently thrilled to receive a note from Monty saying, 'I have yielded all to Christ.'[11]

At the time, both Monty and Stanley were doing trials for the Varsity rowing. Unfortunately, Monty, who was not as good as Stanley, did not get a place and so had to settle for the trial boat. However, Monty worked so effectively on sharing his faith that all the rowers became teetotal and the boat became known as the 'teapot eight'. His prayer was simple: 'May the whole eight become Christians.'

Once Monty had completed his university days, he stayed at Cambridge and moved on to theological college, Ridley Hall, determined to be ordained. However, on 18 October he met up with Stanley at a young men's meeting at the CIM headquarters. Here he picked up a pamphlet, *A Strange but True Story,* which challenged Monty about the claims of the mission field.

The Studd and Beauchamp families were drawn closer together when Kynaston (Studd) announced his engagement to Monty's sister, Hilda.

On 3 November Stanley Smith was invited by Handley Moule, then Dean of Trinity College, Cambridge, to address a meeting of Ridley Hall students and friends on the subject of Holiness. Monty attended the meeting and he took it as a God-opportunity when they travelled by the underground train back to Victoria, and had a serious talk about China.

The next day was a Tuesday. That night, back at the Beauchamp home in Cromwell Road, Kensington, Monty spent time with God, reading his Bible and praying. As he did so, he became convinced that, not only should he go to China, but he had a responsibility to persuade others to do so as well.

The next afternoon, Stanley, CT and Dick (Hoste) travelled together for a series of Christian meetings at the University of Oxford. Monty joined them for the last few days, then travelled on with them to Cambridge for more meetings. Hudson Taylor also joined for what turned out to be a week's mission in the Alexandra Hall, starting on Wednesday 12 November. The Christian Union at Cambridge began to be stirred. As one undergraduate expressed it:

> We have had missionary meetings and we have been hearing missionaries talk to us from time to time. But when men whom everyone has heard of, and many had known personally, came up and said: 'I am going out myself', we were brought face to face with the heathen abroad[12].

Montagu Beauchamp served in China for fifteen years and then served as a chaplain to British forces in the First World War in Egypt and Russia.

William Cassels

William Cassels was born and raised in Portugal where his father was a merchant. On his father's death he was sent to be educated at Repton School in Derbyshire. From there, he went up to St John's College, Cambridge, and in time achieved his BA degree. Despite being older, he and Stanley Smith formed a strong friendship.

He loved sport and was considered a good footballer. If he had not broken his leg, it is almost certain that he would have got his 'blue' in soccer.

After university William planned to take Holy Orders and head out to the mission field with the Church Missionary Society. All who knew him sensed a life of selfless Christian service ahead of him. By nature, he was a quiet, reserved man, which earned him the nickname 'William the Silent.'

In January 1884 William had been working for two years in the crowded slums of South Lambeth, where he was a curate. Here he renewed his acquaintance with his friend, when Stanley helped with a mission in Clapham and South Lambeth. It was during this mission that William and Stanley had 'some arm-in-arm walks and heart-to-heart talks about the Lord and China.'[13]

William found his missionary interest beginning to focus on inland China. But he was not a man to rush things and so continued to pray and seek God. By the August, he was definite about going to China but, when he contacted the Church Missionary Society, he was told they had no plans for working in inland China. William therefore decided to write to Hudson Taylor, and tell him of his interest.

When William's mother heard of this, although she was a believer and had a strong interest in mission, she could not bear the thought of him leaving the UK. She had seven sons and William was the only one still in England. So upset was she at the idea, that she visited Hudson Taylor and pleaded with him not to accept William. He assured her that he would not encourage William if she opposed it. He explained the situation to William and the two of them agreed to do nothing but pray. However, at the beginning of October Hudson Taylor received a letter from Mrs Cassels in which she wrote:

> It is so evident that (William) sees it to be his duty and his privilege to enter upon the Chinese mission work, that I should only take the part of a bad mother to one of the best sons if I continue to put thorns in his sufficiently difficult road … so I must follow, for I could not have led to the course he feels he is led to, and I will try and claim God's gracious promises for him, and for all your work at large.[14]

The path for William to join the China Inland Mission was open before him. The CIM approved his application and the plan at that stage was for William to depart for China in the December with Stanley Smith and Dick Hoste.

William Cassels spent his entire life seeking to win the Chinese for Christ. In time he was appointed the Bishop of Western China. He remained in China until his death in 1925.

Dixon (Dick) E Hoste

Of all the members of the Cambridge Seven, Dixon (Dick) Hoste was the quietest and most unassuming. Yet he was the one who went on to succeed Hudson Taylor as General Director of the China Inland Mission, a position he held for thirty years.

The Hoste family had sixteenth-century Flemish ancestors, who, as Protestants, had had to flee persecution. There was a great-uncle who had served under Vice-Admiral Nelson and done great exploits in the Napoleonic wars, for which he was made a Baronet.

Stanley Smith made friends with Dick's elder brother, William, when he arrived at Cambridge University as a freshman from Clifton School. Theirs was a friendship based on their Christian faith and their interest in rowing. William introduced Stanley to his younger brother, Dick Hoste, who had followed the family tradition of joining the army and was described as 'shy and taciturn gunner subaltern, very recently commissioned, and entirely uninterested in Christianity.'[15] To Dick, attending the garrison church when parade required it, was all the religion he wanted.

Moody's visit to Cambridge in November 1882 stirred many in the Christian union there, including William who had moved from Trinity College, Cambridge, to Ridley Hall to prepare for ordination.

As the term finished and William returned to the family home in Brighton, he was determined to win his younger brother Dick to Christ. When Moody announced a mission in Brighton over the Christmas period, William saw his opportunity. However, Dick had other ideas and refused to have anything to do with it.

Whilst the family went to the meetings, Dick stayed firmly in the drawing room of Havelock Lodge where they lived, reading the newspaper. On the fourth night, William let all the family leave, then firmly said to his brother, 'Come on Dick. Put your wraps on and go with me to the meeting.'[16]

Almost in spite of himself he obeyed. They arrived late and sat at the back. Dick pretended not to be interested but keenly watched all that was going on. When Moody prayed he was astonished as he talked to God as a friend.

Over the next two weeks, Dick said little but attended most of the meetings. He was later to say that he wanted to respond to the message, but worried about the effect it would have on his career, habits and lifestyle.

On the very last night of the mission, Dick slipped into the meeting late and sat at the back. His parents and William were somewhere upfront. When Moody preached and declared: 'Now is the acceptable time of salvation', Dick knew he was right. As the congregation knelt in prayer, Dick resolved to give his all to Christ. A short time later Moody invited those who had received Christ that night to come forward. William and his parents saw the soldiery figure of Dick walking to the front.

In the following weeks, Dick was amazed at the change in his life. Doubts went. Peace overwhelmed him. The Bible came alive. In the eagerness of young faith, he immediately wanted to resign his commission and serve the Lord full time, but his father counselled him to take his time.

Dick expected a lot of ridicule from his fellow officers when he returned to the battery fort at Sandown on the Isle of Wight where he was based. However, he found there was no more than he could deal with. At the same time, he communicated a lot with his brother who was now at Ridley Hall. William shared with Dick about the increased enthusiasm for missionary work spreading round Cambridge and one day he sent him some literature about the China Inland Mission.

By the beginning of May 1883, Dick's father had given him his blessing if he wanted to resign his commission for Christian service and Dick was free to contact Hudson Taylor. On 23 July he wrote: 'Sir I have for some time been thinking about offering myself for the China Inland Mission.'[17]

However, when Dick met Hudson Taylor in August, instead of being welcomed with open arms, he was told all about the dangers and challenges of working in China. A chastened Dick was told to be patient and keep praying.

What none of them knew was that, just a few days prior to their meeting, on 1 August 1883, Dr Harold Schofield had died in Taiyuan, China. It is not therefore surprising that Hudson Taylor spoke as he did. However, God was on the move. They needed to wait His timing.

That waiting progressed a little when, six months later, Dick was interviewed by the CIM Council members. Whilst the Council acknowledged that they thought he would end up working in China, their decision was again to wait. On 15 April 1884 Dick wrote to Hudson Taylor to say his feelings was that he should go to China and he hoped it would be with CIM. In the May he resigned from the Gunners. He planned to use the free time to gain experience of Christian work.

It is known that on 19 September 1884, Stanley Smith, William Cassels and Dick Hoste were together at a CIM function in Aldersgate Street. Dick's acceptance had still not been confirmed but *was imminent*. By 5 November, Stanley, CT and Dick were working together as a team at Oxford University, speaking at a series of meetings. It looked like the three of them would be going together to China.

In 1903 Dick Hoste was appointed to succeed Hudson Taylor as the General Director of the China Inland Mission. For 30 years he led the Mission until he retired in 1935. He remained in China until 1945, when he was interned by the Japanese. He died in London in May 1946, the last of the Cambridge Seven to die.

Cecil and Arthur Polhill-Turner

The Polhill-Turner's home, Howbury Hall in the village of Ravensden, on the edge of the Ouse Valley near Bedford, was a large country house in its own park, to the north of the village. Captain Frederick Polhill-Turner was a Member of Parliament for Bedford and, for a time, the High Sherriff of the County. He and his wife, Emily, had six children, three boys and three girls.

From their early days life was planned out for the children. Schooling for the boys would be at Eton. The oldest child, Frederick, would inherit the estate; Cecil, as second oldest, would enter the Cavalry; and Arthur would be ordained and receive the living at the family church. His faith views were irrelevant as the family assumed he would be taught all he needed to know.

The boys loved their days at Eton and excelled in the new game of football. Arthur was awarded his cricket colours from the more famous C T Studd. Cecil was slightly older than Arthur and went first to Jesus College, Cambridge, as he prepared for army life.

An odd thing – to the boys at least – was the announcement by their elder sister Alice that she was giving up parties and hunting to serve Christ. Apparently, she had been to a church service in Bedford and given her life to Christ.

Much worse was the news in 1881, as Arthur was finishing at Eton and Cecil had just received his commission in the Queen's Bay (2nd Dragoon Guards), that their father had died. He was aged only 55 years.

Despite their father's death, life continued as planned for the children. Cecil joined up with his regiment in Ireland. Arthur went to Trinity Hall, Cambridge. He did as little academic study as necessary, and enjoyed the sport, the hunting, the racing at Newmarket, and playing cards.

As he returned to Cambridge in October 1882, for his second year, Arthur was amused to see posters all around Cambridge announcing that two uneducated Americans were coming to preach for a week. Arthur was amazed when he, and every other undergraduate, received a personal invitation, signed by Kynaston Studd, to hear them speak.

The American visitors became the talk of the town. The first night, Sunday 5 November 1882, Arthur was in the Corn Exchange, to see the fun. There was plenty of rowdiness, clapping, cheering. As the week progressed, the talk of the University was that a lot of people were attending the meetings and strange things were going on. Apparently, some of the rowdy students from the first night, had said their lives had been changed. Arthur visited again on the Thursday night. He had never quite heard the story of the Prodigal Son told so dramatically. Even so when Moody gave the invitation to respond, Arthur did not move.

Back in his room at Trinity, Arthur found himself pondering all he had heard. He wanted to decide for Christ, but knew his friends would ridicule him. He returned to listen to more on the Friday and the Saturday. By the last night, Sunday 12 November 1882, Arthur was in his seat early. He noted all the rowdiness of the first night had gone. As the meeting ended, Moody invited all who had received blessing during the week to stand up. Some 200 or more men, all over the Corn Exchange stood ... including Arthur Polhill-Turner.

Arthur's life was turned around. In an instant, the desire for the theatre, racing, dancing and cards disappeared. He began attending the daily prayer meeting and became friends with Kynastyn Studd, Monty Beauchamp and others.

Back at Howbury Hall for Christmas, Arthur met up with Cecil who was on leave from the Queen Bays in Ireland. Arthur had made no mention of his commitment to Christ. It was as they walked to the parish church that Cecil made some remark about Arthur becoming a vicar. Arthur astounded him because he replied that he was thinking of not taking a living but going to preach in China!

Cecil and Arthur had many discussions – maybe even arguments – about faith during the holiday season. By the time Cecil returned to barracks, he had promised Arthur to try and read a few verses of the Bible each day. If he was honest, his biggest worry was that becoming a Christian could severely impact his relationship with fellow soldiers, and he did not know if he was willing for that.

Throughout the summer and autumn of 1883, Cecil pondered the implications. He had some leave from the army owing to him and so he visited an uncle in Stuttgart, Germany. Cecil used the time to weigh up the call of Christ on his life. When he started his train journey back to Aldershot, his mind was made up. He had yielded all to Christ and trusted in Him.

On 12 November a week of meetings about mission started at Cambridge. Hudson Taylor was the main speaker with CT and Monty sharing testimony. At the final meeting Stanley (Smith) invited any who felt the call to be a missionary, to stand; forty-five stood, including Arthur.

Cecil's expected persecution and ridicule in the soldiers' mess in Ireland when his Christian commitment became known, never happened. His colleagues had always thought him a little eccentric and thought this was another turn of his.

Both brothers were making their own journey as Christians. Feeling an urge for the Far East, Cecil called on Hudson Taylor for advice. They met, talked and prayed, leaving God to clearly show Cecil what was right for him.

On the 8 January 1884, Arthur and Cecil, certain of their call, went up to London to meet Hudson Taylor and offer themselves for China. They were accepted and within six days formalities were complete. Their mother could not stomach having missionary sons and simply told her titled and country friends that 'my sons are travelling in China.'[18]

In 1900, Cecil was sent home to England and forbidden to return to China because of ill health. Even so he made seven long mission visits and, in 1909, he founded the Tibetan Border Mission. He also founded the first Pentecostal Mission society and financed much of the early Pentecostal work in Britain. He died in England in 1938.

Arthur remained in China throughout the Boxer Rebellion and did not leave the country until 1928, when he returned to England. He died in 1935.

Charles T Studd

The final member of the Cambridge Seven was Charles T Studd.

A Move Closer to China?

One day, Stanley Smith – the prize-winning rower from Cambridge and a good friend of the Studd family – was in town and Kynaston and CT arranged to meet him. They knew he was leaving for China in a couple of months' time and wanted to catch up on all his news. They were also aware that other friends, Dick Hoste and William Cassels, had decided to go to China.

When they met, Stanley told them he was going that evening to a meeting at the China Inland Mission headquarters to say farewell to someone who was leaving to travel to China as a missionary. He asked if they'd like to come. CT agreed. It was 1 November 1884.

Afterwards, CT wrote the following account of that meeting, describing the effect it had on him:

> I had never thought of going out of the big country before. I felt that England was big enough for me, but now my mind seemed constantly to run in the direction of the Lord's work abroad. I went one day with my friend Mr Stanley Smith to Mr McCarthy's farewell and I never shall forget the earnest and solemn way in which he told us of how the Lord had led him to go out to China, and the need there was for earnest workers to preach the gospel – how thousands of souls were perishing every day and night without even the knowledge of the Lord Jesus. Then we sang:
>
> *He leadeth me, he leadeth me,*
> *By His own hand he leadeth me;*
> *His faithful follower I would be,*
> *For by His hand he leadeth me.*

And I felt that indeed he was leading me to go to China.[19]

CT did not want to be led by emotion or impulse, and so decided not to make a commitment there and then. He resolved to go away and ask God for guidance. But neither was he one to delay a decision when God was calling. On the way from the meeting, sitting next to Stanley on an open top horse-bus, as it clattered down Essex Road, in London, he told him that he'd decided to go to China. Stanley was thrilled at the news.

However, Charles was not to receive the same reaction when he started to talk with others about his decision. The strongest opposition to his plan was to come from within the family.

Opposition

When next morning, CT shared news with his family that he was thinking of going to China, the family reaction was one of horror. Even his elder brother Kynaston (whose opinion CT respected, deeming him to be a more mature and spiritual Christian) put forth all the reasons why he should not go.

Apart from the family reason Kynaston reminded him he was a well-known and hugely popular sporting personality and that his influence upon the young people of the United Kingdom was considerable. He could do far more by staying in the British Isles and challenging the youth of Britain for Christ than by burying himself away in the interior of China.

Kynaston pleaded with CT to give it more thought, more time, and not to share his plans with his mother until he was sure it was the right thing to do. However, CT was not one to keep things to himself and he knew he had to talk with his mother about his decision.

His widowed mother was still grieving the death of her husband. She had presumed that cricket would occupy CT for a few years and then, when his cricketing days were over, that he would obtain a good job and take care of her. The idea of having a missionary in the family did not fit well with her plans! She was distraught at the idea. As expected, she desperately tried to talk him out of going to China.

A couple of days later, Montagu Beauchamp called at the Studd's home. He wrote:

> I was round there last night and never saw anything like
> Kinny's (Kynaston) depression. He says he has never in his
> life seen two such days of suffering and sorrow, referring to
> his mother … all day she was imploring Charlie not to go
> up to Mildmay (the China Inland Mission headquarters)
> and at all event, just to wait another week before giving
> himself to H Taylor('s work). He would listen to no
> entreaties from Mrs Studd or Kynaston who look upon
> him as a kind of fanatic.[20]

As others in the family heard the news, they joined in the chorus of arguing and pleading with CT. One relative told him: 'Charlie, I think you are making a great mistake. You are away every evening at meetings and you do not see your mother. I see her, and this is just breaking her heart. I think you are wrong.'[21]

CT sought the Lord and was convinced his call was of God. As he read the passage: 'He that loves father or mother more than me is not worthy of me' (Matthew 10.36), he was sure it was God's desire for him to go.

Although Kynaston disagreed with CT's decision, he agreed to come in agreement with him over it and pray with him. In response, CT explained, 'I don't want to be pig-headed and go out there on my own accord. I just want to do God's will.[22]

The two brothers prayed together and put the matter in God's hands. The night after they had prayed together, CT had a restless night, tossing and turning, anxious to make the right decision. It was during those night hours that CT believed he heard the Lord's voice – several times. The voice was reminding him of a verse of Scripture from Psalm 2: 'Ask of me and I will give you the nations for your inheritance, and the ends of the earth for your possession' (Psalm 2:8). He knew what was right for his life. He had abandoned everything to Christ. Even though it was so hard to say no to his mother, he refused to listen to her any more. His mind was made up.

The next day CT arranged to meet Hudson Taylor, the founder and leader of the China Inland Mission and then, on 4 November, he was formally interviewed by members of the Council. Their recommendation was for CT to 'consider the question ... more fully ... and ... if he still wished to go, to write definitely offering himself.' [23] This he did and was taken at his word and accepted.

Those meetings and that decision was to have a profound effect, not only on CT's life, but also on the work of the China Inland Mission. Until that meeting, the Mission, for the greater part of the first two decades of its existence, had been quietly and effectively, but without any great publicity, carrying out its work. The next few months were to see an explosion of interest in CIM, (as it was known), primarily because of CT, but also because of the other six public-school educated young men who offered themselves to serve in China.

The press, both secular and religious, found it a great story that seven young men were going to China, including England's best all-round cricketer, the stroke of the Cambridge boat, a Dragoon guardsman and an officer of the Royal Artillery.

The date of CT's acceptance – 4 November – was just three days after he had gone with his friend Stanley to the valedictory meeting and first heard the call of China. An extraordinarily short time for such an important decision!

However, the pleading of his family did not abate. CT could

see the pain he was causing them, and especially the heartache he was causing his mother. Lady Beauchamp tried consoling her but she was so distressed that she went and visited the China Inland Mission headquarters to talk with Hudson Taylor's wife, Jennie.

As a result of this upset, CT found he had to returning to the Lord for re-assurance on the decision. On one occasion, as he battled his questions and images flashed through his mind of his upset mother, he was standing alone late at night on a station platform. He asked the Lord to give him a Scripture to calm his troubled soul. He opened his New Testament, and under the flickering light of the gas-lamp, he read Matthew 10:36, 'And a man's enemies will be those of his own household.' CT loved his mother dearly but he knew he must obey and was determined that nothing would hold him back.

As news of CT's decision, along with similar decisions by Stanley Smith, Dick Hoste, William Cassels and later Monty Beauchamp became known, interest intensified. Hudson Taylor was due to speak at a series of six meetings at the Alexandra Hall, in Cambridge in mid-November. He was joined by Stanley and CT who explained their decision to go to China. The University had seen nothing like it. To hear the stroke of the Cambridge boat, and the finest all-round cricketer in the country, talk about sacrificing it all for the sake of Christ and departing for far-away China, certainly had the corridors of Cambridge filled with chatter!

On one of the evenings, after Hudson Taylor had given the invitation for those present to offer themselves for missionary service, forty-five young men filed to the front of the meeting. The following night another twenty similarly responded.

Cambridge University students did not know what to make of it and the challenge of Christ became the talking point of university life. During the day CT and Stanley spent their time speaking with individual students. The under-graduates could not help but be impressed. Not only were these young men giving up worldly prospects, but they were doing it with such enthusiasm and gusto.

The commitment of the Cambridge Seven to give up glittering opportunities to go as missionaries caught the public imagination. It was a time when so much store was placed on social position and athletic achievement. Yet here they were, all under twenty-six, with the youngest Arthur Polhill-Turner not quite twenty-two. As far as other students were concerned, they were giving it all up to go and hide away in China. In the history of Christian mission, no group of volunteers had quite caught the imagination of the Church, the universities and the nation at large, as this group.

The normal circulation of the CIM magazine, *China's Millions,* was twelve thousand copies. For the edition carrying the Cambridge Seven's stories, it was decided to print 50,000 copies. That was not enough to meet demand. Their stories were republished in book form – *A Missionary Band* – with pictures and maps, expanded to 250 pages with extra articles from leading churchmen and public figures of the day. The first edition of 10,000 was sold out in a few months. A second edition was published and then a third. Queen Victoria accepted a copy of the gilt-edged edition[24] and other copies were circulated through the YMCA's of Britain and the United States.

CHAPTER 5

Leaving for China

Farewell Meetings

It was an elderly evangelist living in Liverpool, Reginald Radcliffe, who first suggested to Hudson Taylor, that because CT and his friend Stanley had such an effect on students, their departure to China should be delayed so they could challenge the young people of the United Kingdom to yield their lives to Christ. Invitations were pouring in to the CIM headquarters asking for the two of them to come and speak at churches, universities and meetings.

Hudson Taylor decided he could not put off his own return to China but that it was right for members of the Cambridge Seven to delay leaving. It was therefore agreed that they should tour the country and challenge their listeners about their response to Jesus Christ and the needs of the mission field.

On 26 November 1884, CT and Stanley spoke in the Melbourne Hall, Leicester. The pastor of the church, F B Meyer, was to become a famous preacher and teacher, though at the time he was largely unknown. He was thirty-seven and had already held pastorates at Pembroke Baptist Chapel, Liverpool, and Priory Street Baptist Church, York. In the late 1870s he had gathered a group of Christians together to build a new Church in Leicester. It was known simply as Melbourne Hall, Leicester.

The meeting on the 26th was crowded and many were challenged about their Christian walk. None more so than the minister himself. Later Meyer recalled, 'I saw these young men had something which I had not. What ... was within them was a constant source of rest, strength and joy.'[1]

At seven am the next day, in the grey mist of a November morning, Meyer paid a visit to CT's and Stanley's lodging and found they had already long been at their Bibles, reading by the light of a flickering candle. When they invited him in:

Meyer commented to CT 'You have been up early.'

'Yes,' said Studd. 'I got up at four o'clock this morning. Christ always knows when I have had enough sleep and He wakes me to have a good time with him.'

Meyer asked: 'How can I be like you?

CT enquired of Meyer: 'Have you ever given yourself to Christ, for Christ to fill you?'

'Yes,' said Meyer, 'but in a general way. I don't know if I have done it particularly.'

The talk that they had, Meyer called: 'one of the formative influences of my life.'[2]

There was nothing new in what Meyer was told but, as he listened, he was reminded that a man must not only believe in Christ for final salvation, but must trust Him for victory over every sin and for deliverance from every care ... and must then wholly yield to

Him. A new fire touched Meyer's heart and quickened all he did from that day forward.

CT and Stanley departed for Scotland on 28 November, only twenty-eight days after CT had first heard the call of China. The trip was to continue until the 9 December. CT took nothing with him but the clothes he had on. His mother was very upset to receive a note from Hudson Taylor asking her to put a parcel of clothes together and send it to CT. She responded: 'How or why he should wear one shirt night and day till the 9 December is a mystery to me when he has a supply provided and one has always been taught that 'Cleanliness is next to Godliness'.'[3]

She asked Hudson Taylor to appoint an older mature Christian to oversee him once he arrived in China. This clearly was a matter of concern to her, for she wrote to Hudson Taylor's wife, Jennie, on the 5 January: 'A few lines to ask you to impress on him (CT), the necessity of taking what is necessary to be comfortable.'[4]

Their first meeting in Scotland was on CT's twenty-fourth birthday, 2 December, at Glasgow University. Then on to Greenock, Dundee and Aberdeen. Their host in Aberdeen, Major Ross, later told the General Assembly of the Free Church of Scotland that he had been praying for years for his sons to become ministers of the gospel, and two of them had done so following CT and Stanley's visit.

They arrived in Edinburgh on Tuesday 9 December. A group of medical students had undertaken to organise the event. Afterwards, one of the students wrote a report on the meeting.

> We resolved to do Christ's work in every detail in the
> best possible style. To this end we asked the University
> printers to have our notices printed on good paper and

in good taste. All our hymns were carefully chosen and well printed, and each hymn sheet had the university crest embossed upon it. We hoped the students would take them home and keep them.

We hired the Free Assembly Hall, because we expected a crowd. We decided students only should be admitted, and put it at the bottom of the notices.

For several days before the meeting we had a number of 'sandwich men' with large posters walking in the neighbourhood of the University and the Infirmary. We committed ourselves to great things. Our prayers were answered far above our asking. Twenty minutes before the appointed hour men were rushing up the steps of the Assembly Hall, asking if there was room.

CT and Stanley had arrived at lunch time and spent the afternoon in their host's drawing room in prayer till they got the victory (for the evening meeting). Nearly all the gentlemen invited to join them in praying came and, before they went into the Hall, they all knelt in prayer for God's blessings. Meanwhile the students in the Hall had been singing their usual 'before lecture' songs and beating time with their sticks.

As soon as CT and Stanley entered they were loudly cheered. We had made it plain in our notice that they were going to China as missionaries, and our men had come to hear what Studd, who had made the biggest score at cricket in Cambridge, had to say about religion. They admired their consecration.

Again and again during their addresses, they were cheered. Stanley Smith was eloquent, but Studd 'couldn't speak a bit'. It was the fact of his devotion to Christ that told, and he, if anything, made the greatest impression. Professor Charteris was in the chair and he announced that if any would like to shake hands with them, and wish them God-speed, they could come forward as soon as the Benediction had been pronounced.

All the men there were students and we wondered who would have the courage to do so, but no sooner had the Benediction been pronounced than there was a stampede for the platform. A great impression had been made, and many were crowding around Studd and Smith to hear more about Christ. A great religious movement had had its birth.

They were leaving for London by the 10.30 pm express so they could attend the wedding of Kynaston Studd to Hilda Beauchamp the next day. We walked down to the station with Studd, and when we got to the Waverley Station platform, we found that a number of students (100 or more) had gone down to see them off. As soon as they caught sight of Studd, there was a cry of 'speech' and Studd had to stand on one of the seats and address them still further.

We overheard a gentleman asking a porter, 'Who are these?' The porter replied in Scots Doric: 'Th're aa medical students but th're aff their heeds.'

As the train moved off, some ran up to the end of the platform cheering.'[5]

The next day, amidst all the enjoyment of the high society wedding between Kynaston Studd and Montagu's sister, Hilda Beauchamp, there was much chatter about all that had been happening in Scotland and their soon departure to China. Gradually a plan emerged for a nationwide evangelistic tour by CT and Stanley to reach the youth of the United Kingdom with the message of the gospel. Hudson Taylor was in total agreement with the plan and gave his blessing to his new recruits to delay their departure.

Christmas Day saw CT, along with Stanley and William Cassels speaking at the YMCA headquarters in Aldersgate Street, before dashing back to their respective homes for Christmas dinner with their families. On the 29th the three of them were in Brighton for two meetings arranged by Dick Hoste, another of the Seven.

The first time all seven were together on the same platform was on 8 January 1885 at the Exeter Hall, as they supported Hudson Taylor before his departure for China. The hall was 'absolutely packed'.

The following day, CT and Stanley travelled on the 1.30 pm train from Euston to Liverpool. There they met the elderly Reginald Radcliffe and addressed a meeting of 1,200 young men. Stanley wrote: 'Such a time of power. Many received Jesus. Young men broken down. … this is the Lord's doing.'[6]

The three of them travelled on to Scotland – Aberdeen, Banff, Huntly, back to Aberdeen, Montrose and then Perth. Stanley wrote in his diary of the Perth meeting: 'About one hundred and fifty stopped to the after-meeting, and I believe there were many souls won.'[7]

On Saturday 17 January, they arrived in Edinburgh and spent the day in prayer with members of the University Christian Union for the meetings planned for the next day. The Sunday afternoon saw CT and Stanley addressing some thousand 'upper class boys' in the Free Trade Hall. Then it was on to the United Presbyterian Synod Hall, Edinburgh's largest hall, for an evening meeting. It held over 2,000 people and was packed.

The Christian newspaper, on 19 February 1885, included an article by Dr D A Moxey, a Professor at Edinburgh University, about the meeting.

> The event that has precipitated the shower of blessing that has fallen in our midst, is the recent visit of the two young Christian athletes from Cambridge, who are now on their way to preach Christ to the Chinese. Students, like other young men, are apt to regard professional religious young men of their own age as wanting in manliness, unfit for the river or cricket-field, and only good for psalm singing and pulling a face.
>
> The big muscular hands and long arms of the ex-captain of the Cambridge eight, stretched out in entreaty, while he eloquently told out the old, old story of redeeming love, capsized their theory, and when Mr C T Studd, whose name is to them familiar ... as perhaps the greatest gentleman bowler in England, supplemented his brother athlete's words by quiet but intense and burning utterances of personal testimony to the love and power of a personal Saviour, opposition and criticism were alike disarmed, and professors and students together were seen in tears, to be followed in the after-meeting by the glorious site of professors dealing with students and students with one another.[8]

What the newspaper accounts didn't record was that, at the end of the meeting, those who wanted to 'consecrate themselves to the service of God,' were invited to stay to an after-meeting. Half of those present stayed. A few more words were spoken and then CT and Stanley went down amongst the men anxious about their souls.

The next day there were long lines of men queueing outside 50 Queen Street, where they were staying, for an interview with them. "Each one was limited to 15 minutes during which time they were each asked if they wished to become a Christian and then prayed over. They rose full of joy, having received their salvation."

The newly-saved then shared the good news with others and many more made commitments to Christ, including many who followed the pattern of the Cambridge Seven, and gave up promising careers in order to serve the Lord.

On the Monday afternoon CT and Stanley had a meeting at the Free Assembly Hall, chaired by the great hymn writer, Horatius Bonar. The evening was a repeat of the Sunday night with another packed hall, a deep work of God and many personal conversations. It was clear the spirit of God was using the two young athletes from Cambridge.

Stanley's diary records the events of the next few days: Clydeside: 'God came down in power'; Greenock: 'God came down'; Rutherglen: 'Souls converted and delivered'; Alexandria: 'God fell on the audience'.

They had been asked before leaving Edinburgh, if they could come back. Their only free day before moving on to meetings in England was the Friday of that week. As they arrived, the organisers told them of students who had been converted the previous week, who had gone out seeking their friends and bringing them to Christ.

The meeting was the most remarkable of their time in Scotland.

Three to four hundred students stayed to the after-meeting. At 10.30 pm, the hall was still strewn with men anxiously enquiring about their soul. One of the committee asked the hall manager for an extension of time and it was agreed until midnight. CT and Stanley were humbled at what God was doing.

After Edinburgh a series of farewell meetings around England had been organised. Wherever they went – Newcastle, Manchester, Rochdale, Leeds, and many more places – the meetings were packed.

The meeting in Manchester on 26 January, saw a thousand – nearly all young men – stay to the after-meeting.

CT wrote to his mother two days later: 'We had a grand meeting at Rochdale. They say there has never been such a meeting there before. The hall was crammed. We had a huge after-meeting. It was like a charge of dynamite exploded among them.'[9]

On the Thursday, 29 January, they were back where their tour had started in Liverpool. They had a brief rest at Reginald Radcliffe's home in Waterloo, and then their final meeting at the YMCA. Before departure from Liverpool's Lime Street railway station at eleven in the evening, CT rushed off a note to his mother: 'Splendid news from Liverpool: The fire is still burning and over sixty professed conversion on the one night. I cannot tell you how much the Lord has blessed us … cricket and racquets and shooting are nothing to this overwhelming joy.'[10]

But his eyes had been opened to scenes his privileged life had hidden from him before. In another letter to his mother he wrote:

The poor in London and all great towns has increased my horror at the luxurious way I have been living; so many suits and clothes of all sorts, whilst thousands are starving and perishing of cold, so all must be sold when I come home, if they have not been so before. God bless you dear darling mother, and I know He will do it, and turn your sorrow into joy.[11]

Mrs Studd did as CT requested and disposed of his 'goods and chattels' and sent a cheque to the CIM. However, she didn't grasp fully what he was saying. After CT left England on 5 February to sail to China, it emerged that his mother had sent a case on ahead of him, with instructions it was to be unpacked before he arrived, so his room would be ready for him with 'curtains … knives and forks, table napkin etc.'[12] If it ever arrived, it was never mentioned again!

By the time CT and Stanley returned to London, Hudson Taylor had already departed for China. Not for Hudson Taylor the glamour of the crowds. He had a work to do in China. From the midst of the China Seas he wrote:

Soon we shall be in the midst of the battle, but the Lord our God in the midst of us is mighty – so we will trust and not be afraid. He will save. Some months later he wrote: Flesh and heart often fail: let them fail! He faileth not. Pray very much. Pray constantly, for Satan rages against us.[13]

The Cambridge Seven came together for the China Inland Mission's London Farewell meeting on Friday 30 January at the Eccleston Hall. They then stayed together until departure, except for a rushed visit to Bristol by CT and Stanley, where the Colston Hall was not large enough to hold everyone who wanted to attend.

In their final week, there were three more meetings for the Cambridge Seven– Cambridge, Oxford and the day before departure at the YMCA's newly refurbished Exeter Hall in the Strand. At each meeting all seven spoke. John Pollock described their different abilities on a platform:

> Smith would seem severe, though affectionate and charming on closer acquaintance; Studd's gentleness almost belied his burning words; Beauchamp, with his enormous frame and somewhat florid face and his capacity to extract enjoyment from anything, was almost as eloquent as Smith; but Hoste and Cecil Polhill-Turner were shy and found public speaking a trial. Cassels, as quiet as Hoste, as good a speaker as Beauchamp, was in many ways the most mature of them all. [14]

The Cambridge Correspondent of the *Record* newspaper wrote of the meeting in the Guildhall, Cambridge on 2 February:

> By far the most remarkable event of this week in our religious world has been the meeting of 'farewell' to the China Inland Missionaries in the large room at the Guildhall. Very soon after 7.30 the great hall was crowded in every corner, floor, orchestra, and gallery. Quite 1,200 persons must have been present, including a very large number of gowns-men.
>
> Professor Babington took the chair, and his presence was a very valuable testimonial of confidence in a devoted spiritual enterprise, on the part of a leading representative of science. ... one after another, the new missionary volunteers spoke with very different degrees of eloquence, but with beautifully uniform simplicity in stating their motive and hope, and confessing their Lord's names and claims ... it was the most remarkable missionary meeting held within

living memory at Cambridge and it has stirred hearts deeply, far and wide.[15]

The next night, the Seven were in Oxford where the Corn Exchange, the largest hall in the city, had been booked. It was filled to overflowing, with many left standing for the entire meeting.

Their final meeting was the day before they sailed, at London's Exeter Hall. Such was the impact that the Cambridge Seven had made on the nation, that the national dailies, including the *London Times* gave extensive coverage to it. The day was a miserable one with 'sheets of rain.' The worry of the nation concerned General Gordon and what was happening in the Sudan, in Africa.

Crowds attended, filling every space, including the platform, galleries, all the nooks and corners. Then the lower hall was filled, and a hurriedly arranged overflow. It was the largest of all their meetings. CT's mother managed to get in, as did his brother Kynaston and his new wife. So many wanted to be present that some had to be turned away.

On the platform were forty Cambridge undergraduates. They sat in front of a large map of China. Once the meeting began the Seven were introduced to the audience, with roars of cheers and clapping. Stanley addressed the main hall whilst CT went down to the Lower Hall. Stanley touched on the emotion of the day when he referred to General Gordon of Khartoum, not knowing he was already dead: 'A greater than Gordon cries from Khartoum ... the voice of Christ from the cross of Calvary.'[16]

When CT had returned to the main meeting and it was his time to speak, he shared frankly about his conversion and backsliding before his brother's near fatal illness. 'I had formerly as much love for cricket as any man could have ... but after yielding to Jesus Christ as LORD ... my heart was no longer in the game.'[17]

He finished by challenging his audience: 'Choose who is to be your God – the true God or your own substitutes. Then obey Him.'

The meeting concluded with the organist striking up the music for Frances Havergal's great congregational hymn: 'Take my life and let it be consecrated Lord to Thee.'

None of the Seven really understood the influence that their actions were having, and would continue to have for generations to come, on the history of mission. A great wave of missionary zeal swept through the student bodies across the land, from Edinburgh, to London, Oxford and Cambridge. Only God knows the impact CT and other members of the Seven, made on the young people present at the meetings. Many, many lives were touched. No records have been kept but some went on to have great influence and impact in the Kingdom of God.

The CIM magazine, *China's Millions*, in 1885, listed the qualifications looked for to be a missionary with the China Inland Mission. They stated:

1 We have no inflexible educational standard

2 A fair English education

3 Good health

4 Plenty of common sense

5 Well ascertained success in mission work at home.
   If a person has not proved themselves at home a
   successful worker, they are not likely to do it in China.

6 The qualification needed above all is, full consecration
   of heart and life to God, true love to the Saviour and the
   souls of men.

A note of caution was added:

> We want to be sure that those who go, are called of God to the work and fitted for it … If you join the mission, you must bring enough faith into it, to keep yourself, and then it will not be the poorer but the richer for your coming into it. [18]

CT spent his final night before departure at the family home in Hyde Park. He hardly slept, knowing his life was about to change for ever. Would he be able to hack it? If his father was alive would he approve? Would his mother in time accept his decision? So many questions. The next day would be the start of a new life for him.

CHAPTER SIX

China at Last

Departure Day

On 5 February 1885 the newspapers were full of the news of the surrender by the British of Khartoum, the capital of Sudan and the death of General Gordon, who was leading the British forces, killed by followers of the Mahdi in Khartoum. Queen Victoria was still on the throne. Britain ruled its Empire. China was going through major upheaval.

The Cambridge Seven met up at Victoria Station, London, to begin their journey to China. As they boarded the Boat train, due to depart at 10.00 am, they were surrounded by a host of friends and relatives, many in tears at their going, wondering if they would ever see them again.

Some of CT's friends from the MCC team were there to see him off. Such was his popularity that some of them travelled on the train with him to Dover and even over the Channel, before saying their final goodbyes. Kynaston, with his new wife, along with his mother-in-law Lady Beauchamp, did the same, accompanying them as far as Calais. Cassels, the oldest man in the party – a month short of twenty-six – pasted labels on all their luggage, which said: *God first.*

Right on time the train's whistle blew and clouds of smoke billowed from the engine, as the train departed Victoria Station amidst shouts of encouragement and good-byes. The last person CT could pick out in the crowd, as he frantically waved from the train window, was his sixteen-year old sister, Dora, with her bright blue dress. As the train sped through the English countryside the Seven had plenty of time to ponder on what might lie ahead of them. CT used the time to write long letters to his mother, describing all the details of the journey.

Accommodation on board ship was not quite what these young pubic-school educated aristocrats were used to. CT wrote:

There were seven second class passengers (fit only for servants and dogs … and by a special deal, offered to CIM at a twenty-five per cent discount[1]) and we trust that all are now God's own children. The case of one is truly marvellous.

The man is a captain of an Indian steamer and had been noted for lying, drunkenness, swearing and blasphemy. Well thank God. He has brought even this man to know Jesus as Saviour. Hoste began to talk with him the first day, then somehow, one afternoon the Lord led me to go and speak with him about his soul. He seemed softened and I urged him to decide at once. On his knees in his cabin he cried to God to forgive him and received the Lord Jesus as his Saviour. He has three times publicly given his testimony. His whole life has changed. Most of the day is taken up with reading the Bible. Praise the Lord! It is lovely. Not only have these been brought to the Lord, but also several of the stewards. You can imagine what a change that means among the ship's company.[2]

After the captain, several of the crew responded, as well as some of the second-class passengers. On they travelled, via Brindisi in Italy, Alexandria, Egypt, then through the Suez Canal, and Colombo. They had to change ships at Colombo, in Ceylon (Sri Lanka) where they held a number of meetings. Then on to Penang in Malaysia, Singapore and Hong Kong.

When the Seven weren't witnessing to the passengers and crew, they attempted to learn the Chinese characters. The captain gave them permission to hold services on the quarter deck and most of the passengers, both first and second class, attended. Openly the young men invited the passengers to give their lives to Christ. At the ports the ship stopped at, they disembarked and sought every opportunity to share Christ.

Arriving in China

As the ship docked in Shanghai on 18 March 1885, the Cambridge Seven saw a man on the quayside frantically waving at them. They didn't recognise him. It was only as they came down the gangplank that they realised it was Hudson Taylor, in Chinese dress. He had come to the quayside to greet them, having arrived earlier to arrange for their induction course and onward inland travel.

However, before the course, a series of meetings was arranged in Shanghai where the Seven could reach out to the British and

European community. Shanghai was a Treaty Port, which meant it was open to foreign trade and thousands of Europeans lived there. The Temperance Hall was the largest venue available so that was immediately booked. The impact of the Seven on the Shanghai community was the same as it had been in the UK. After the first day, there was not even standing room to hold all who wanted to attend. Interest in the meetings was increased when local newspapers such as *The Shanghai Mercury* carried sympathetic reports of them.

One amazing story out of those meetings was from the British chaplain, Rev Fred Smith, who was in charge of the Anglican Cathedral in Shanghai. He came forward after CT had spoken and confessed that, if he had been called home by the Lord the night before, he would have been a lost soul. Those who knew his story were aware that he had been brought up by pious parents who taught him the Bible and arranged for him to be confirmed and then later ordained into the Church of England. He confessed to the meeting that he had tried to be a good Christian but had never committed his own soul to the Lord. He ended his little speech by declaring: 'Now ... I am the Lord's and He is mine.'[3]

All seven of the new missionaries stayed in the CIM hostel in Shanghai during their time there, attending the induction course that Hudson Taylor had arranged.

One of the first things they had to learn was how to dress. It was traditional at the time for foreign missionaries to keep wearing the clothes they usually wore in their home country. Hudson Taylor, however, disagreed. He felt suits and ties in the midst of China was off-putting to those hearing the gospel. So, much to the displeasure of other missions in the foreign settlement who wanted to preserve their British ways, all male missionaries with the China Inland Mission shaved their heads and started wearing pigtails … and this was the requirement for the Cambridge Seven.

Too much mirth from the new arrivals, the seven new missionaries abandoned their trousers and shirts, and started wearing Chinese-style skirts and long-sleeved gowns. When, subsequently, the women CIM missionaries followed suit and wore Chinese clothing, other missionaries thought it scandalous! Whatever would their mothers think of them?

CT wrote home to his mother to tell her about it:

I have been laughing all day at our grotesque appearance … we put on the clothes this morning, were duly shaved and pigtailed … Monty, Stanley and I make huge Chinamen. It makes us very conspicuous, as Chinamen are short. Stanley makes the best Chinaman. Monty is far too red-faced and looks most comic.

In another letter dated 23 April, he wrote:

This is the first walk I have had in Chinese dress which even approached to comfort, for Chinese feet are small, whereas you know mine are large, and I could not get a pair of shoes large enough. The first shoemaker called in said he had never made such a pair as I wanted and fled the house, utterly refusing to undertake such a gigantic operation. However, another was found. He said he had made many pairs of shoes, but never made such a pair as these. It is often a great joke amongst the people, and the Chinamen often point and have a good laugh at them in the streets.

Not all was fun and laughter. In a letter dated 26 May to his younger brothers Reggie and Bertie still at Eton, he wrote:

> We were over-run with rats who, during the night took away our socks, nibbled away our legging tapes and took away our blotting paper to use in their nest ... We thought of setting traps, but decided not to do so and simply ask the Lord to rid us of the grievance. Since that time, we have had no further trouble with them.[4]

After a few months in the comparative luxury of Shanghai, it was time for them to move into the interior. Hudson Taylor's original plan was to keep the Cambridge Seven as a unit, and have them working together in the great province of Sichuan. It was a huge area some 600 x 500 miles and teeming with millions of industrious people, but in the end, Hudson Taylor decided: 'discretion required a careful approach. Seven young athletic men, including two of undisguisedly military bearing, could arouse misplaced suspicion.'[5]

The Seven were split into two teams of three with Montagu Beauchamp remaining with Hudson Taylor to travel with him. Stanley Smith, Dick Hoste and William Cassels were sent by ship, via Yantai to Tianjin and on through Peking to Shanxi, there to learn Chinese and join the work of missionary David Hill's convert, Hsi, who was known as Xi Liaozhih, and was becoming a remarkable leader.

With CT were the two Polhill brothers and John McCarthy, as escort-interpreter. They were assigned to the north, to Pinyang and Tai-yuan. It was a difficult journey by mule, foot and houseboat with plenty of mud and sleeping in dirty Chinese inns. At one stage CT's feet became so bad that he took off his sandals and walked bare feet. But that only made them worse.

A typical day's pattern for CT would be: Wake up at 2.00 am to read his Bible by candlelight, until 3.30 am. Then he would pack and prepare for leaving at 4.00 am. The group would aim to walk eight miles before stopping for breakfast. From then on, it was walking, eating and resting, then more walking, until it was time to stop for the night. The aim was to walk forty miles in a day.

In one of his letters home CT described one Saturday's travels:

> On Saturday my companions (two colporteurs) were anxious to do the journey quickly and bent on doing 40 miles. This was not a bright look-out with my feet. They wanted to get me a horse but could not. So bad were my feet that it seemed an impossibility to do such a distance; but the Lord did enable me, how I do not know. It was very painful indeed, and of course my feet got worse. Next day 38 miles. Uuh! Each step was like a knife into them, but I never felt the Lord's presence nearer the whole time. I was mostly alone, especially the last days as I could not keep up with the others. But I thank the Lord for it all, for he has taught me so many, many lessons by this suffering.

His feet clearly were an issue. On 19 October from Singan CT wrote again about his feet:

> I asked Hogg if he would anoint me with oil in the name of the Lord, (according to) James 5.14-15, as I believed the Lord would heal my foot. He hesitated at first, but we read James 5 together and prayed about it, and he said he could see no reason against it, and did so. Since then my foot has got rapidly better. Next day in faith I took it as being well (though it looked anything but so) and walked

a good deal on it. It was much less swollen at night. I have continued to do nearly 20 miles a day on it since, with the result that it has lost all its swelling and is fine on the sound one and there is no discharge. I do praise the Lord for this.[6]

Much of CT's time was taken with trying to get to grips with the language. He found it so frustrating not being able to speak one word of Chinese that the people understood. He was supposed to be a missionary and yet could not communicate with the people!

Much to Hudson Taylor's dismay, CT and the Polhill brothers became so frustrated at their lack of ability to communicate with the Chinese people and their own slowness at grasping the language that they decided to follow the Biblical way of acquiring a foreign tongue.

> On the slow journey up the Han River they put away
> their books and gave themselves to prayer for a Pentecostal
> speech in Chinese ... Arriving eventually in Hanzhong, they
> persuaded two of their young missionary women to do
> the same.
>
> But before October ended they saw their mistake,
> knuckled down to study, and in time became fluent.[7]

That was one thing less for Hudson Taylor to worry about!

CT also learnt important lessons on travelling light and being a one-book person. From this time on, it became a principle of his life to read the Bible, almost to the exclusion of other books.

In a letter he wrote from Pingyang on 7 February 1886 he gave an insight into the secrets of his spiritual life:

The Lord is so good and always gives me a large dose
of spiritual champagne which braces one up for the day
and night. I generally wake about 3.30 am and feel quite
awake, so have a good read and then an hour or so's sleep
before finally getting up. If I miss this time, I feel like
Samson shorn of his hair ... I see how much more I have
to learn of the Lord. I want to be a workman approved,
not just with a 'pass' degree. ... What a life the Spirit lives
out in us when he possesses us. It is so simple too; just
remember 'I have been crucified with Christ'. I am dead. It
is no longer I who live but Christ that liveth in me.[8]

They finally reached Pingyang on the 3 November 1885. It had
taken seven months since they left Shanghai. CT allowed himself
a little longer in bed once they settled in the city.

Not all other missionaries and missions in China took to the
Cambridge Seven. For some they were just too enthusiastic with
their faith. Frederik William Baller had been in China with the
China Inland Mission since 1873 and was considered one of their
most experienced missionaries. But he wrote that he was repelled
by their extreme piety. Stanley Smith and Hoste in his opinion
were damaging their health by excessive prayer and fasting.[9]

By the May (1886), CT was in Chin-Wu and spending time
alone there. This forced him to try his hand at communicating
in Chinese with those around him. Two months later, he was in
Tai-Yuan for a conference and had an opportunity of meeting
up with some of the other Cambridge Seven and hearing of their
adventures. Unfortunately, however, one of the other missionaries
caught small-pox, meaning that Monty and CT missed most of
the conference attending to his nursing needs.

In the August, CT journeyed from Tai-Yuan to Hanchung with Hudson Taylor. On reaching the outskirts of the city they heard that riots had taken place in surrounding areas, all foreigners had had to flee and many houses had been destroyed. CT and another missionary, John Phelps, immediately volunteered to go into the city – it was a scary journey.

The Consul of Chungking, a Mr Bourne, could not believe it when they arrived since guards were supposed to be on all the city gate to keep out the 'Foreign Devils' (as foreigners were called). He wanted them to leave immediately but CT told him that God had brought them there and they would stay. After a few days John Phelps departed but CT stayed in the Consulate using his time to contact local Chinese Christians and encourage them in their faith.

He stayed there for several months and, to his amazement, one day a large, thick envelope arrived for him from the bankers, Messrs Coutts and Co.

Inheritance

CT knew that, according to the terms of his father's Will, he would receive an inheritance when he passed his twenty-fifth birthday. With all that was happening in China, he had forgotten his birthday had been and gone.

The package, which had managed to find him at the Consulate in Chungking, was to inform him the terms of his inheritance. Copies of the stocks and shares and money he had inherited were contained in the envelope. When CT added it all up, it totalled £29,000 – a huge sum of many millions in today's terms. Certainly, it would be sufficient for CT to live comfortably for the rest of his life.

Here he was giving everything up to serve the Lord in China with a mission that was 'living by faith and praying in its finances.' What was he to do about his inheritance?

CT was well aware of Bible passages, such as Christ's words: 'Lay not up for yourselves treasures on earth' (Matthew 6:19). He knew that Christ had told the rich young ruler: 'Sell what you have, and give to the poor, and you will have treasure in heaven; and come, take up your cross and follow Me' (Matthew 19:21).

CT's father had died two years previously so he had had plenty of time to consider what to do about his inheritance. His mind was made up. The right thing for him to do was to give all of it away, apart from a small reserve in case of future marriage. However, since he could do nothing about the money whilst he was stuck in the middle of China, he decided to ask his brother Kynaston to agree to become power of attorney for him and distribute the money. But how could he arrange that when he was stuck in the middle of China?

As ever, God had put CT in exactly the right place. Since he needed a British official to sign documents so that the necessary authority could be given to Kynaston, CT approached the Consul. Unfortunately, however, at first the Consul didn't want to sign. He couldn't understand why he would want to give all his money away. Was he sure? Didn't he want to think about it? In the end the Consul said he would sign the necessary papers if CT would wait two weeks, and then come back to him with the same request.

CT was sure and so he used the next two weeks to plan who the money would go to. One of his first gifts was £5,000 to Dwight L Moody, the man responsible for his father coming to the Lord. He hoped that Moody would use the money to begin an evangelistic work in Tirhoot, India, where CT's father had made his fortune through indigo dye. In the end, this was not possible but Moody was able to use the money to start the famous Moody Bible Institute in Chicago which trained people to take the gospel throughout the world, including to India.

Since CT had a heart for the poor and was aware of the work that George Müller was doing in Bristol, caring for homeless children through the orphanages he had founded. He therefore donated £5,000 to Müller, with a request that £4,000 be spent on missionary work, and £1,000 among the orphans. Other cheques for the same amount were sent to George Holland, a preacher working amongst the poor of Whitechapel, London, asking that it be 'used for the Lord among the poor in London.' Holland had been a spiritual help to Studd's father and CT asked for the receipt to be in the name of his father.

A cheque for a similar amount was sent to Commissioner Frederick Booth-Tucker, General William Booth's son-in-law, who was responsible for the Salvation Army's work in India. This particular donation arrived immediately after the Salvation Army had held a night of prayer for reinforcements, and they used the money to send out fifty new officers.

The remainder of the money was allocated to a number of missions and Christian charities on CT's heart, including Miss McPherson for her work in London, Miss Ellen Smyly in Dublin, Rev Archibald Brown in the East End of London, Dr Barnardo's Home and to the China Inland Mission to help with the cost of sending out new workers. On 13 January 1887, with the necessary papers in place, and signed off by the Consul, all the paperwork was sent off to his brother.

According to CT's sums, by the time he had finished, he would have just £3,400 left in his bank account at Coutts.

CT did not give the money away with the idea he would ever receive anything in return. Money was never an issue for him. His personal needs, both on the mission field and at home, were minimal. As he gave away his inheritance, he could never have imagined that, in his lifetime, he would receive a hundred-fold back the money he had given away, through those who gave to his mission.

Norman Grubb wrote about this principle of absolute faith that CT expressed:

> C T Studd had the simplest of simple faith. In years gone by, when a young man, he gave all his money away in one day. With the last gift of £2,000 he cracked one of his little jokes. He wrote to General Booth of the Salvation Army, 'Henceforth our bank is in Heaven.' You see we are rather afraid — notwithstanding the great earthly safety of Messrs Coutts and Company and the Bank of England — we are, I say, rather afraid that they may both break on the Judgement Day. It seems to us that heaven is the safest bank, and it is so handy; we have no trouble about cheques or rates of exchange, and just 'ask and receive, that your joy may be full'. [10]

For the next thirty years, CT proved God's faithfulness financially.

With the inheritance distributed, and other missionaries who had fled Chungking during the riots beginning to return to the city, CT decided it was time for him to make his way to Shanghai. He had heard that his brother George was on a ship coming into the port and he wanted to be there to meet him.

George in China

In April 1887 CT arrived back in Shanghai, from the interior, and booked himself into the China Inland Mission guest house. He was so looking forward to seeing his brother George again and catching up on all the news from home. Also staying in the CIM guest house were Miss Black, a spinster lady who was the guest house hostess, John Stevenson the deputy director of CIM and Priscilla Stewart, who was a CIM missionary who was too ill to travel into the interior.

CT knew that George was travelling to avoid the severity of the English weather, which affected his health, and that the ship he was on was stopping in Shanghai. He understood that George was only staying for a short time and then travelling on.

CT arrived in the city, two weeks before George's ship arrived in the port. Unfortunately he was unable to do any work amongst the Chinese there since the dialect was quite different from that of the west and the north where he had been working.

The Shanghai port was busy with ships of Her Majesty's Navy and so CT used the time waiting for George by holding nightly meetings in the Shanghai Sailor's Home, a guest house for sailors who came into the port.[11] When George finally arrived on 19 May, he shared a room with CT at the CIM guest house. The day after he arrived he booked the next stage in his travels – on a ship leaving for Japan a week later.

CT knew that George had become lukewarm in his faith but made a point of not talking with him about Christian things. They talked about family. George was able to update CT and tell him that his baby sister Dora was now married and that Kynaston was the proud father of a new son.

George used the first few days to play cricket at the local English club. He ran up a large score which attracted attention, and the interest grew and grew when CT went to watch. People began asking why he was not playing and why he had given everything up for his religion.

What CT did not know was that George was watching him … and God was working in his life. The day before he was due to leave Shanghai on the next part of his journey, George made a dramatic return to God and announced it very publicly at one of the meetings they attended.

George never did catch the boat that week bound for Japan. Instead he travelled with CT into the interior. Sometime later, he told CT: 'If you, Charlie, had tackled me on religion when we were rooming together (in Shanghai), I should have sailed in that boat to Japan.' CT's response was that 'the leadings of God are not infrequently mysterious but always perfect!'[12]

In a letter sent to his mother, dated 27 May, George wrote:

> You will see by my writing thus that a change has come
> over me, and I know it is just in answer to prayer; for
> Charlie had got Mr Stevenson, Mr McCarthy and others
> to prayer for me before I came, that I might … surrender
> willingly to the Lord Jesus Christ. And ok, I have felt
> the Spirit striving within me, and I felt such a hungry,
> unsatisfied craving that I could not rest till I had given
> myself up, and now I can't tell you what peace and joy the
> Lord has given me in believing.[13]

CHAPTER SEVEN

Two Shall Be One

Priscilla from Ireland

The growth of the China Inland Mission was amazing. From its beginnings in 1865, it had grown to 225 missionaries and fifty-nine churches in China by 1883 . That number was to explode in 1887 when another 102 recruits travelled to China to join CIM. The Mission actually had 600 men and women offer for service, of which 102 were chosen, equipped and sent out. They became known simply as *The Hundred*. One of their number was a missionary from Ireland called Priscilla Livingstone Stewart.

Priscilla, or Scilla as she was known to her friends, had been born on the 28 August 1864. She had grown up in a wealthy home in Lisburn, Northern Ireland, and exuded her Irishness, both in her looks, her energy, and in her spirit with blue eyes and golden hair. It was said her hair was like her father's and her petite build had come from her mother.

Priscilla clearly showed in lifestyle that she had no time for Christianity, or for religious people, even though the family described themselves as Anglican. 'People who go to church have faces as long as a coffee pot,' was one of her favourite sayings![1] Her lifestyle exuded what she thought having fun was all about.

Once, when out for the evening with some friends, they dared her to smoke six cigarettes, one after the other. Not wishing to be beaten, she took up the challenge, smoked, and won. Eternity had no fear for her. She openly declared: 'I will never serve God. I will never love Jesus nor call Him Lord and Master.'[2]

God, however, had other ideas. Two of Priscilla's uncles became believers. This resulted in their becoming an embarrassment to the rest of the Stewart clan, as they sought to share their faith and encourage them to convert.

One night Priscilla dreamt that Jesus was standing before her and telling her to depart from him. She was arrogant enough to laugh and tell him that that was fine as she would have a wonderful time in hell with her friends. But as she looked around, she saw she was alone and the picture of hell frightened her.

Priscilla was not one to worry too much about dreams until the night she had another one in which she saw Jesus, bloodied and dying, hanging on a cross. He was saying, 'With my stripes you are healed.' She didn't really understand the significance of the dream but it unsettled her.

When she told a friend about it, she tried to prove to her and others that God was not in dreams.

'I can prove it,' she said. 'If I eat things which disagree with me, they disturb my digestion, and when I sleep I dream … God had nothing to do with my dream. That was the result of a supper of champagne and lobster and whirling round a ballroom all night.'

However, Priscilla's words didn't even convince herself. Before the end of the day she was on her knees committing her life to Christ. Telling the story later she said:

I realised that I knew the devil as a person, as he actually seemed to come to my side, torturing me by bringing to remembrance all the times I had mocked and scoffed and said I would never love God nor yield my allegiance to him.

At the end of quite a time a gentler influence seemed to overshadow me and a voice, oh so different, asked: 'Child what do you want?'

'To get to God,' I replied, 'but I can't, for there seems veritably a great gulf fixed and, like Bunyan, with so great a load on me, that I cannot move.'

(Suddenly close to Priscilla was raised the Cross of Jesus Christ, with Christ nailed upon it, and a crown of thorns upon his brow.) I saw the wounds and riven side and I saw the blood flow.

I asked 'Why wast thou there?'

A voice immediately replied: 'With my stripes you are healed.'

(The vision of the cross disappeared, her burden too, and she arose. Priscilla had not realised it but she had been on her knees two hours.)

(Priscilla's friend asked her,) 'Well what is it to be?'

I replied: 'I have seen Calvary and henceforth he shall be my Lord and my God.'[3]

How her life changed! The effects of the 1859 Ulster revival were still being felt in Ireland at that time. She joined the Salvation Army. There were lots of processions in the streets, hymns being sung, open air meetings being held, and men and women preaching. Priscilla loved to join in especially the Salvation Army processions. She rejoiced in being despised for the love of Jesus – even when ridicule was thrown at her, as well as stones, old shoes, oranges and bad eggs.

Previously some of the youths in the community sought her company because of her good looks and personality. Now they would walk on the other side of the road and pretend not to know her or greet her. She didn't care. She had found Christ which compensated a thousand times for anything she had lost.

In 1887 the China Inland Mission issued a rallying cry for one hundred new missionaries, willing to give everything up and serve God in China. It seemed an amazing request for a mission that was only twenty-two years old, but it came out of a time of prolonged prayer and fasting by the first meeting of the Mission's China Council. So confident was Hudson Taylor that God would answer prayer that, at the Annual Meetings in London on 26 May 1887, he declared: 'We have been led to pray for one hundred new workers this year. We have the sure word, 'Whatsoever ye shall ask in My Name, I will do it, that the Father may be glorified in the Son.''

One hundred new missionaries would represent rapid growth in administration, in finances and in the work. As the call went out, the Home Department began to sift through the paperwork of almost six hundred candidates who applied.

At the same time the income of the Mission rose from £22,000 to £33,700, and that without any appeal. Eleven contributions alone supplied no less than £10,000. There was thus little extra strain imposed on the financial department

In time the six hundred who applied were whittled down to one hundred and one of those selected was Priscilla Stewart, who had sensed the call and applied to join the Mission. Two years after the Cambridge Seven had responded to the call, a further hundred including Miss Stewart sailed to China. The year was 1887.

Once in Shanghai, Priscilla, along with the other new candidates, went through the induction course. For six months they were trained in the language, etiquette, geography, Chinese religion, how to communicate the gospel, and all the things that you needed to learn about a new country. The plan was that, at the end of the six months, the hundred would be distributed around the interior of China. For Priscilla, the plan was for her to accompany three other women to an inland mission station in the city of Ta-Ku-Tang.

As the training course came to an end, the leadership in Shanghai were concerned Priscilla's health would not survive the interior. It appeared her heart was not up to the stresses of missionary life. To her deep disappointment she was told to hold back in Shanghai.

Once the others had departed, she used her time to assist Miss Black, the CIM guest house hostess, and the CIM Deputy Director, Mr Stevenson. She began to attend the meetings at the Sailors' Guest House and it was there that she was introduced to CT. CT's initial reaction of her was not to be impressed.[4]

Mr Stevenson asked CT one evening for his opinion on Priscilla. His response was that 'she has made a mistake in coming out for she seems as though the life has been eaten out of her, and she could never stand the interior. It seems a real labour for her to get upstairs.'[5]

It was the time when CT was in Shanghai to meet his brother George. Whilst waiting he was leading meetings at the Sailor's Home. One day he decided to read out a letter that he had received from Booth Tucker of the Salvation Army, thanking him for his financial gift. In the letter Booth Tucker told CT that his gift had enabled fifty Salvation Army officers to be sent from England to work in India. He described what it was like for the team in their work:

> Life was hard but they were seeing many souls saved. He wrote about one area where 'a simple Scottish lass and a rough native servant girl took charge of a (Salvation Army) hall, and in two months one hundred souls were added. Never before had native women been known to speak in public.'[6]

He also described how these warriors had no salaries, receive no money, and had learnt to be there – 'with content'. No grumbling or arguing were heard in the camp.

> For meals (he wrote) they have rice water in the morning, rice and vegetable curries (no meat) at mid-day and the same in the evening. The use of tea and coffee is quite given up as being too European! … Most beautiful of all has been the spirit of unity, love, devotion and sacrifice which has animated them all from the first.
>
> Remember (he wrote) that mere soul winning is comparatively easy work and is not nearly as important as that of manufacturing the saved ones into Saints, Soldiers and Saviours. [7]

All who listened as the letter's content was read out, had their souls stirred. It challenged them about their lifestyle and attitude. Priscilla had been present at the meeting and she decided to become a regular attendee at the daily meetings at the Sailors' Home.

The meetings did not have much structure and anything could happen. CT assumed responsibility for the meetings and, in time, Priscilla also took the lead. As the meetings progressed, CT described them as 'becoming hotter and hotter.' By now he was becoming impressed by Priscilla and was to say when she spoke, her messages were 'all fire, the fire that burn into people's souls.' On another occasion he described them as 'real hot and cram-full of joy.'[8]

At most meetings, including those when Priscilla spoke, sailors got converted and went back to their ship, to tell what happened and invite the men to come to the meeting the next night.

The unorthodoxy of the meetings is illustrated by a time when they wanted to express joy. CT announced the hymn, 'Stand up, Stand up for Jesus'. It dawned on him that almost everyone was already standing up, so he shouted; 'Stand on your chairs for Jesus'. The sailors jumped on their chairs grinning from ear to ear; the Sailor's Home had never heard the hymn sung so vociferously. Everyone was on their chairs, including Priscilla Stewart – except for one man who was a missionary. He happened to escort Priscilla home that evening and told her in no uncertain terms that standing on chairs was bad manners, and 'most improper, very irrelevant, and made a ridicule of religion.'[9]

At one of the meetings Priscilla shared the story of her conversion and calling to China. Through that, one of the ladies present asked if she would come to her house and share her testimony. When Priscilla arrived, the lady had organised for a group of her friends to be present to hear her story of how her life had changed and her calling to China. The meeting took the form of a tea party. Soon Priscilla was being invited to tea parties around Shanghai, where Christian ladies would invite their friends for tea and to listen to Priscilla share her story.

CT's brother, George, wrote about Priscilla to his mother in a letter dated 3 June 1887:

> There is a Miss Stewart here who has been lately coming to the Mission and has been wonderfully used of God. Doors have been opening to her right and left, and in several houses, she has been the means of bringing people to their knees in drawing rooms, where I do not suppose anyone ever knelt to the Lord before. Truly the Christian life is a happy one when it is all for Jesus.

As Priscilla took every opportunity of sharing her story, a physical change was also taking place within her. Whereas previously she had struggled to climb a few stairs, now she could bound up the stairs three at a time.

There came the day when it was decided that Priscilla was fit enough to be posted to work in central China. She took the journey alone, travelling on a steamer to one of the Treaty Ports on the Yangtze River. It was night time when she departed Shanghai.[10] In the morning she found one of the other passengers on board the ship was none other than the missionary who had scolded her for improper behaviour when she had encouraged the sailors to stand on their chairs for *Stand up, Stand up for Jesus*. As they talked, he admitted that she and those like her had a different religion to his. Priscilla challenged him.

Here CT picks up the story as Priscilla told it to him.

'Are you willing to do anything for Jesus? If you are willing to do anything for Jesus the same as we are, God is no respecter of persons, and will surely give you the same joy that wc have.'

'Well,' he said: 'I don't know that there is anything that I would not do for Jesus. I admit that I refused to stand on the chair for Jesus, and I don't seem to have had much peace since that incident.'

'Well,' Miss Stewart continued. 'I think I should get rid of that if I were you.'

'But,' he said, 'what can I do? There is no meeting here.'

'If I were you, I should stand on a chair for Jesus.'

'What!' he said, 'Here on the ship?'

'Yes,' she replied. 'Right here on the ship.'

This young (missionary) doctor was lost in thought, but he meant business, so presently he got up and went into the saloon and stood on the chair for Jesus. Whether he sang, or merely read the hymn we do not know, but we know he returned from the saloon a different man from the one who entered it.[11]

Marriage

A week after Priscilla was posted by the China Inland Mission into the centre of China, CT, with George accompanying him, left to work in the north. The last thing on Priscilla's mind was marriage. She was fiercely dedicated to the work the Lord had for her in China and didn't want any romantic relationship to get in the way of the calling. However, once they had both left Shanghai, a lively correspondence began. The first letter that hinted at anything more than mutual friendship – certainly on CT's side – was dated 9 June 1887.

Very quickly CT had become convinced they were meant for each other. He had said nothing whilst they were together in Shanghai but, in a blunt and unromantic way, CT told her by letter: 'You have neither the mind of God nor the will of God on the matter, but I have. And I intend to marry you whether you will or not, so you'd better make up your mind and accept the situation!'[12]

Quite what attracted CT to Priscilla is open for discussion. He had difficulty describing her to his mother and in one letter wrote: 'Oh, I know one thing more; her name is Priscilla Livingstone Stewart and she calls herself 'Scilla' (rum name ain't it?). Why not Pris, I don't understand but then she is 'Irish".[13]

Later in life he wrote:

I am quite sure my wife must have been good looking for everyone said so, and she always remained extraordinarily young looking. She was like a volcano and I have often said: 'Never spake a woman as this woman.' ... She spoke not from books, nor from the study, nor from the meditation, her speaking was from vision and communion. What she believed she saw, and as she saw so she spoke, and for that reason had such an effect on her audience.[14]

CT tells the story of sitting talking with another missionary in Tai-yuan one afternoon when the missionary congratulated him on being engaged to the prettiest girl in all of Shanghai. CT's response is fascinating for he said he was shocked for he had never thought of her pretty face. 'I verily believe that of all God's many good gifts the least of all is good looks.'[15]

In fairness to CT, what he was trying to say was that he was not marrying her for her pretty face (though she might have had that), but marrying her for her love of the Lord Jesus Christ and her love for those whom He had sent her to serve.

Priscilla did not play easy to catch! She kept all his love letters to her. One was nearly seventy pages in length![16] In one, dated 25 July 1887 he wrote:

> But here I do say that after eight days spent alone in prayer
> and fasting, I do believe the Lord has shown me that your
> determination is wrong and will not stand, and that you
> yourself will see this presently, if the Lord has not shown
> you already.[17]

Although they had not seen each other since Priscilla had been posted to central China, they became engaged at the beginning of October 1887. Several days later, in one of his letters to her, CT wrote:

> Now before I go further I do want to beseech you darling,
> that we make the same request every day to our Father,
> that we may give each other up to Jesus every single day
> of our lives, to be separated or not, just as He pleases, that
> neither of us make an idol of the other.[18]

Years later CT was to write:

> My wife possessed an extra-ordinary personality, wherever
> she went everybody seemed to confide in her … on one
> occasion we went to America together. She was always
> very careful of my health, so when the Sunday came, she

would not let me speak more than once, but the people insisted there should be a second meeting, so she had to take it, and took it to such effect that not a few were visibly affected as she spoke of our work in China. It became the talk of the ship.[19]

Before they could be married, however, both fell dangerously ill; Priscilla with pneumonia, after kneeling in the snow to pray for souls at an open-air meeting, and CT with pleurisy in both lungs, typhoid and then pneumonia.

On 26 December 1887 Charles received a letter from one of Priscilla's co-workers to say that Priscilla was seriously ill. He didn't know it at the time but the well-known Chinese evangelist Pastor Hsi had been visiting the four lady missionaries on their station. They had asked him to take an open-air meeting right outside their home. The snow and sleet were falling. The street was running with water. Even so the ladies, including Priscilla, knelt on the ground praying for those listening. The result was she had a bad attack of pneumonia. She was so ill that some of the other workers feared she might die.

Remembering how poorly Priscilla had been in Shanghai, CT equally was worried that the pneumonia could be fatal. He reckoned if he travelled night and day he could reach Priscilla in three days. He set off immediately, praying all the way. By the time he reached her she was over the worst.

They were able to spend time together, talking and praying and reading the Scriptures – something they had not had time to do previously. A few days after CT had arrived in Hoh-chau, Stanley Smith reached the city.

He and CT almost immediately departed to journey back to

north China. As they journeyed Stanley became poorly, suffering from typhoid fever. For the next three weeks CT nursed him, whilst using the time to think about Priscilla. He became convinced that there was no reason to delay his marriage to her. He wrote and shared with Priscilla what he was thinking. In one of his letters CT wrote:

> I am for being registered at the Consul's and then having a real Hallelujah meeting, just something all for Jesus. We are strangers and pilgrims here, and I vote we have a real pilgrim's wedding.

When Stanley was well enough, instead of carrying on journeying north, they turned around to return to Hoh-chau.

Their arrival was a shock to the church there, though Priscilla was delighted. In Chinese culture it was thought wrong for an unmarried man and woman to look each other in the eye, let alone travel for days together. So, when CT and Priscilla announced plans to travel together to the nearest British Consul at Tientsin so they could ask him to marry them, the Christian converts in Hoh-chau were horrified. CT and Priscilla understood and decided to have a Chinese wedding in Hoh-Chau – but without the smart wedding clothes.

In later life, CT loved to shock his friends and acquaintances by claiming to have been married twice. When they heard him they were shocked and would whisper 'Who is the other woman?' His response was always the same. 'Married twice but only one wife. Thank God.'

Their first wedding day was at Priscilla's mission station with Pastor Hsi officiating. It was not a 'real' marriage but CT and Priscilla felt they should do it to please the Chinese and help the cause of evangelism. On the day, they married in their everyday Chinese clothes (to the disdain of their friends), with Priscilla wearing a long white sash with the words 'United for fight for Jesus' on it.

Pastor Hsi insisted that CT wore a new hat and a pair of shoes which he gave him. After a feast at the mission house, they left for the coast, where they were officially married before the British Consul at Tientsin on 7 April 1888. Until the 'official wedding' they lived apart.

Besides their wedding vows, they also made a special vow to each other, and entered into it as a contract with God, that neither would keep the other back from doing any work that God laid on their heart that they must do.[20] That vow was to be challenged many times in their married life.

When they arrived in Tientsin for the wedding, a letter was waiting for CT from the family solicitor. All the money he had been left in the inheritance, had been distributed as instruct. There was just £3,400 left in the account. What did he want to do with it?

Just before their wedding CT presented to Priscilla the money, as a wedding present. Her response summed up the character of the wife C T Studd was marrying:

'Charlie, what did the Lord tell the rich young man to do?'
'Sell all,' he replied.
'Well then,' she told him, 'we will start clear with the Lord at our wedding.'[21]

Together they proceeded to give the remainder of the inheritance away. In a letter they sent to General Booth at the Salvation Army, they started by expressing how blessed they had been through reading General and Mrs Booth's addresses in the *War Cry* newspaper and in their books. Then they wrote:

> And now we want to enclose a cheque for £1,500 …
> Another £500 has gone to Commander Tucker as a
> wedding present. Besides this I am instructing our Bankers,
> Messrs Coutts and Co, to sell our last earthly investment
> of £1,400 'Consols' and send what they realize to you.
> Henceforth our bank is in heaven …[22]

CT incorporated in the letters verses of Scripture including:

> Sell all that you have and give alms (Matthew 19:21)
> If you love me keep my commandments (John 14:15)
> Make for yourselves purses which wax not old.
> (Luke 12:33)
> We thank God that we are in that proud position …
> 'Silver and gold have I none' (Acts 3:6) … we don't want
> to be like Ananias and Sapphira.

Their worldly possessions on their wedding day were 'five dollars and some bedding.' With an unwillingness to spend any money given to them on anything other than essentials, there was the issue of a wedding ring. When Priscilla had left Ireland for China, a friend had given her a simple gold band. Inside the band, were the letters 'CTS' stamped on it. That became her wedding ring for the first eight years of married life.

There is an interesting story of how, years later, when they had left China and returned to England, CT's mother asked Priscilla one day where her wedding ring was and she showed her the simple gold band the friend had given her. His mother was shocked that she had no proper wedding ring. When

Priscilla explained that 'Charlie says he will never buy any other,' Mrs Studd replied with 'Alright, you shall have his father's mother's wedding ring!' With that she got it and put it on Priscilla's finger.[23]

Start of Married Life

Once married CT and Priscilla were assigned to open up a new work in the inland city of Lungan-Fu (now called Changzhi), in Shanxi province. With them in the work was a fellow missionary and friend of Priscilla, Miss Mary Burroughes.

As a unit, they were determined not to live amongst other Europeans but to be part of the Chinese community. However, they found that renting anywhere was difficult. The only house available to them was one that no one else wanted because it was said to be haunted.

Life was not easy for the newly-weds. Try sleeping in a bed infested with scorpions! Financial support was slow in coming. Food was constantly in short supply. Much worse was that their neighbours did not like having western Christians near them and shouted curses at them when they left their house – every day – for five years.

Whenever anything bad happened in the city, the Chinese blamed it on the 'Foreign Devils' in their midst. They thought nothing of standing outside the house and peering through the windows. CT, Priscilla and Mary were objects of ridicule whenever they went out. In China the custom for a husband and wife, when out walking, was for the wife to be three steps behind the man. CT and Priscilla wanted to show they were equal, and so walked side by side, as the watching crowds mocked and mimicked.

A time of crisis came when the region faced a drought. Inevitably the Foreign Devils were blamed and accusations made against them that the rain gods did not approve of them being in the area. The Mandarin, who ruled the city, put out an order that on a certain day, all businesses were to close and everyone was to place burning incense outside their homes as worship to the rain god. The three missionaries knew that there would be trouble. They prayed fervently.

On the day in question, a procession of town people processed around the city, carrying a stone statue of the rain god. It was around midday when the procession reached near the Studd's house. Their doors were locked. They could hear the chant of the crowds:

'We want rain. We want rain. Kill the Foreign Devils. Kill the Foreign Devils.'

There was a banging noise against the back wall and the three missionaries smelt acrid smoke. The building had been set on fire. Others were attacking the Mission house with picks and axes. Suddenly out of the crowd a Chinese scholar appeared and shouted at the crowd.

'Stop wasting time. Attend to the rain god's needs, not a house.'

Quickly the men dropped their axes and picks and took up the large stone statue again and marched off towards the market. CT stood with his head bowed, thanking the Lord for saving the three of them from the mob and death.

CT and Priscilla gradually began to learn that evangelistic methods which worked in the West were not necessarily the way to do things in China. As a result new ways were found and people began to relax and started to talk with them. CT and Priscilla began to see fruit from their labours. The power of the gospel began to work in the hearts of the people.

One man they witnessed to many times, confessed that he was a confirmed opium smoker, and had broken every commandment in the Holy Book. He believed he was beyond the redemption of God. CT therefore spent time with him explaining what the death of Christ on the cross meant and how God's offer of grace through Christ ensured he could be forgiven. The man received God's forgiveness and, as happened to the evangelist Philip when he explained the message of salvation to the eunuch in Acts 8, the man immediately requested baptism. Once baptised he left the city to return to his village.

The man wanted to share the gospel with the people there and to ask forgiveness for the wrong things he had done. Crowds came to listen to him. But when he confessed some of the wrong things he had done, he was taken before the Mandarin who ordered him to be lashed 2,000 times with the bamboo.

He was left for dead. Friends took him to a hospital, and he was nursed back to life. Disregarding advice, he returned to his city. This time the authorities were too ashamed to give more bamboo strikes so sent him to prison.

However, when they learned what had happened, people gathered near his cell, which had an open window, with bars, to listen to him preaching. In the end the authorities let him go and he spent his time sharing the gospel and the change it would bring to lives.

Delights of Having Children

As the birth of their first child approached in 1889, the Studds had a great deal of heart-searching to do. They were in the midst of rural China. No doctor or nurse was within six days' travel of them. Their choice was to stay or to go! They could leave their post three months before the birth date so that Priscilla could have the benefit of a doctor at her disposal. It would also mean remaining away for a further two months after the birth, when she would be strong enough to travel back.

CT and Priscilla could not contemplate five months away from their work and decided their trust must be in Dr Jesus. Both had been given two months' basic nursing training at the Queen Charlotte Hospital in London before they came out to China. They also had two medical books with them but, as neither of them covered the subject of giving birth, they were not much use!

As so often happens in child birth, their first child arrived unexpectedly. Priscilla had to act as mother-to-be as well as doctor, whilst CT took on the role of nurse. Stanley Smith was visiting them at the time so he retreated into the next room to pray. A baby girl (Grace Faith Salvation) was born healthy and well. Several days later, a lady missionary, Jessie Kerr, who was trained as a midwife, came to visit them, and relieved CT of his responsibilities. (Mary Burroughes had left by then).

However, a few days later Priscilla started haemorrhaging. Their concern turned to seriousness, and then alarm. The day came when Jessie Kerr came to CT to tell him that Priscilla's condition had deteriorated rapidly. 'I fear I ought to tell you that I can give her no hope of her recovery,' she declared. 'Death is looming.'

Much prayer had already been made for Priscilla. Now, CT realised, was the time for specific prayer and anointing. He therefore leant over his wife and whispered, 'Would you like me to anoint you and pray?' She nodded assent and CT anointed her in the name of the Lord.

The next morning when Jessie Kerr arrived, she went in to see Priscilla and take charge. When she reported that she had found a remarkable change in his wife, CT's response was that anointing and prayer was 'the only way you will ever live in China.'

Four more children were to follow – three girls: Dorothy Catherine (1891), Edith Mary Crossley (1892), and Pauline Evangeline Priscilla (1894); and one boy, Paul Snowball (1890) who lived just one day. Priscilla never saw a doctor through all the births. The family remained in China seven more years after the first baby was born.

Priscilla believed that the Lord gave her four beautiful girls as a lesson for the Chinese people. Years later she was to write:

> One of the curses of China is not to let their little girls live. They say they have trouble bringing them up and then when they are married, the dowry they receive does not make up for all that has been spent on them. I went into a mother's house once and found her groaning. I (knew she had just given birth and) asked where the baby was. It was born at daylight and immediately had been thrown into the moat or into the pagodas which are built for this purpose, with a certain hole, so that the wolves can jump in and get the baby when they want it. How many times have I come home broken?[24]

CT and Priscilla deliberately named their first girl Grace, their second Dorothy which means 'praise', followed by Edith (meaning 'prayer') and the last one Pauline ('joy'). The Chinese thought CT very strange to call a daughter 'joy'![25]

Our God Will Supply Our Every Need

It was one thing to claim the Lord supplies all your needs when you are a famous cricketer in England and there is money in the bank account. But what do you do when you have no money … and no supplies … and are in the Chinese heartland with no one to tell? There came a time when all of CT's and Priscilla's supplies ran out and there was no hope of supplies from any human source.

The mail was delivered once a fortnight. One evening, having put the children to bed, Priscilla came to CT's room and said, 'We have to look facts in the face. If the return of the post man brings no relief, starvation stares us in the face.'

They decided to have a night of prayer. They got down on their knees and began to pray. After twenty minutes they stopped. They had told God everything. They could not think of anything more to say to God. Charles wrote later:

> It did not seem to us either reverence or common sense to keep on talking to God as though he was deaf or could not understand our simple language or the extremity of our circumstances, or the weight of the words of His Son who had said that God knew everything before we told Him, and as He said Himself, 'Before they call I will answer.'

The mail man returned at the appointed time. CT and Priscilla eagerly opened the mail bag. There were some letters but they knew by looking at them they contained no money. They picked up the bag again and shook it. Another letter fell out. It must have been stuck in a corner. They did not recognise the handwriting and thought nothing of it.

Lazily we opened it and began to read. How different we

were after reading that letter to what we had been before
… and I think our whole lives were different.

As CT looked at the letter, he saw a signature that was unknown to him. This is what he read:

> I have for some reason or other received the command of
> God to send you a cheque for £100. I have never met you.
> I have only heard of you but that not often. But God has
> prevented me sleeping tonight by this command. Why
> He should command me to send you this money, you will
> know better than I do. Anyhow, here it is and I hope it will
> do you good.

CT and Priscilla had never seen or corresponded with the man before. The letter had been written many weeks before and been on its journey to China.

Years later, CT was at a meeting in Manchester and told the story. The man who had sent the letter and the cheque was there. He came and introduced himself to CT after the meeting. His name was Frank Crossley.[26]

Gradually the work CT and Priscilla were doing began to grow. Stanley Smith and his wife came and joined them in Lungan-Fu. One of the biggest needs of the area was reaching out and helping opium addicts and so this became their focus. As the work grew, funds were made available to them from the UK to enable them to purchase a larger property in the area. Pastor Hsi also came and joined them and in time they were able to help fifty addicts at a time. They were encouraged. As God blessed the work, lives were changed, and addicts set free.

CHAPTER EIGHT

On the Move Again

Leaving China

In 1894 CT's health became so bad that the family decided they had no choice but to return to England. Neither CT nor Priscilla kept a diary, but Priscilla had scribbled on some sheets of paper during the previous year:

> March 27 1893 – Charlie very ill today – seemed as if the Lord about to take him. We did all we could to relieve him but in vain. About 4.30 pm he asked to be anointed. A group of eight or nine gathered at his bedside and anointed him. About 12 pm breathing lighter and better. Morning much better.[1]

Priscilla's health equally was not good.

Soon afterwards a letter arrived from CT's mother. She had heard from others how bad their health was and was offering to pay for the family to have a break in the UK. In faith she sent the money to cover their travel expenses. CT wasn't so sure and decided to pray about it … for six months!

Once they decided to leave, they handed over to the China Inland Mission the buildings they had bought, and severed their links from the Mission.

Departing China was very different from how CT and Priscilla had arrived. Ten years earlier they had set foot in the land, as single people, full of vision and excitement for what lay ahead. CT had been fit, agile and a sporting hero, and Priscilla lively and enthusiastic in her love of Christ. Now they were both returning home broken physically with four children who only knew of China as home and knew no English.

Their departure was very different. They knew it was a closure to future work in China. They were now a family unit and so needed to plan for the children as well as themselves. It was a long journey to travel to the coast and then catch a ship back to England.

As they left the village they had lived in, people flocked out to say their goodbyes. They did not dare ask the two Chinese nurses who had helped look after the children to accompany them to the coast with them for fear the people would think they were stealing them, and taking them to the land of the Foreign Devils. There was still many who viewed them with suspicion.

The journey was a mixture of sedan chairs on mules, cargo boats on the river and sleeping on top of boxes. It was a time when Japan and China were at war and the majority of the Chinese people were uneducated about who was fighting who. To many of them all Foreign Devils were on the side of the Japanese.

At one stage of their river journey near to Tientsin, things got rather ugly as a huge crowd gathered to see the Foreign Devils. It was their young girls, speaking Chinese, talking to the crowd that calmed matters for them.

Once they arrived at Shanghai, they boarded a German Lloyd steamer and travelled second class home.

China had been wonderful but also challenging. CT especially was a free-thinker and being part of a disciplined team was not easy for him. He was undoubtedly a pioneer and longed at times to be able to do his own thing. He thus found submitting to others not easy. But life had not been all bad. CT and Priscilla had met each other and been blessed with four wonderful daughters.

Return to England

The England of 1894 was a very different and surreal world from what the family had left behind in China. The four girls could only speak Chinese and were accustomed to Chinese ways. Grace, Dorothy, Edith and Pauline were now about to be faced with new customs, a new language, new relatives, new ways of dressing and new temperatures. It was not just the girls who faced new situations. Priscilla had never met any of CT's family and could only imagine the 'posh' lifestyle they lived. As the family stood on the side of the deck watching the fore-line of England come into view, it was hard to imagine what was going through their minds.

Kynaston was at the quayside waiting to greet them on a cold winter's day. CT and his mother were greatly devoted to each other and she would not hear of them staying anywhere but with her at her Hyde Park house. She was so excited to welcome him and Priscilla, and meet her grand-daughters for the first time that she wanted to spoil them all by buying everything that money could buy.

Not only did she insist on housing them but wanted them all to have the latest fashion in clothing. In China they had all been wearing Chinese garments. They had tried hurriedly as they were leaving China, to buy western clothing in Shanghai but, as far as his mother was concerned, they were poor quality and ill-fitting.

She sent CT out with Kynaston, by then the Lord Mayor of London and living in the Mansion House in the City of London, to buy several new suits. The two of them drove in his mother's carriage to the various stores. As they were travelling back from the stores, Kynaston turned to him:

> Well old chap, we don't know quite how you are situated
> for funds, but certain rumours have been about which
> suggest that your bank balance is not quite as fat as it used
> to be. It would be a help to us to know just how you stand.
> Of course, I know that mother paid your passage home
> which probably helped a bit, I don't suppose you'd object
> to let me know what balance you have got.

When CT told the story, he said:

> I put my hand in my pocket and produced five bob
> and I shall never forget his face. He said nothing but he
> gave a little whistle, and a whistle can sometimes be very
> expressive.[2]

To enable CT and Priscilla to meet old friends and make new ones, his mother had appointed a nursemaid for Pauline, the youngest child and a nanny to look after the other three girls. The children had never seen anything like it before. The house had a cook, a butler and two housemaids, and the girls watched in amazement on their first morning as the maids tidied up the grate, then laid and lit the fire.

The relationship between staff and children was not an easy one. On one occasion one of the girls was naughty and the nurse decided to punish her by locking her in the bathroom. The other three girls kept tugging at her skirt and speaking very fast in Chinese until the nurse relented and unlocked the bathroom door.

CT's mother insisted that the family had medicals to check their health issues. This revealed that Priscilla's heart condition was worsening, affected most probably by giving birth to five children. It was also discovered she was pregnant again. The doctor told CT he had developed chronic asthma, but thankfully not tuberculosis. The girls were all given good bills of health. When the new baby was born, for the first time Priscilla had a doctor present. However, sadly, despite the presence of medical aid, the baby boy was weak and sickly and only survived for two days.

CT's mother and brothers were concerned at CT's pecuniary state and how he was going to provide for his family. Kynaston used connections with the Regents Street Polytechnic to obtain the position of Chaplain for him. But that was not the route that CT wanted to go.

CT was to suffer from ill-health for the rest of his life but he would not let this interfere with his desire to tell people about the gospel. As soon as he felt well enough, he accepted invitations to speak from universities and many other events across the United Kingdom. His fame had not diminished and the crowds flocked to hear him. He began to travel and share throughout the country. It was not just in public meetings that CT would share the gospel. He did so in one-to-one chats, though sometimes not in an orthodox way.

On one occasion, whilst holding a meeting in Wales, he upset his cousin, Dollie Thomas, by comparing faith to smallpox. She could not understand what CT was going on about when he said to her: 'If you get it, you give it to others and it spreads!' As they chatted, she offered him a cup of cocoa, but he rudely left her holding it out as he talked. When she got angry – as a Victorian lady was allowed to do – he told her: 'That is exactly how you are treating God, who is holding out eternal life to you!' Two days later he received a telegram that read simply: 'Got the smallpox badly – Dollie.'[3]

News Year's Day 1896 saw CT in Liverpool for a conference of a thousand university students from twenty nations. The theme of the five-day conference was mission. It was out of this conference that the committee of students adopted as their watchword: *The Evangelisation of the World in this Generation.*[4]

February 1896 saw CT and an American, A T Pierson, hold another conference for students, under the Student Volunteer Movement banner (a movement that his brother Kynaston had helped to found – see below). One of the attendees was C S Rolls, an undergraduate of Trinity College, Cambridge. He had just purchased the first car seen in Cambridge and only the fourth in the United Kingdom. It was during the conference that Rolls shared he had become a Christian.[5] He went on to be the joint-founder of Rolls Royce and the first person to fly a non-stop double air crossing of the English Channel.[6]

The Student Volunteer Movement in America had grown

from a summer Bible conference conducted for college students in North America in 1886. It had been hosted by Dwight Moody and sponsored by the Young Men's Christian Association (YMCA) which, at that time was openly evangelical in outreach and orientation. Moody had invited Kynaston to speak during a tour of America that he had organised and to tell the story of the Cambridge Seven. The revival that CT and Stanley Smith had seen in Britain before they departed for China, had spread to America.

A gentleman called John Mott was asked to lead the new movement.[7] His name may not mean much to today's generation but John Mott went on to become one of the most influential missionary mobilizers in world history. His conversion had happened a few years earlier. He had arrived late for a meeting Kynaston was speaking at. Flustered, at disturbing the meeting, the man was hit with the words: 'Young man, are you seeking great things for yourself? Seek them not! Seek first the Kingdom of God!' He was so challenged by the words that the next day he gathered the courage to meet and talk with Kynaston. He was later to describe that time as 'the decisive hour of my life.'

America on Tour

In October 1896 CT was invited on a preaching tour of America. As he departed, leaving an unwell Priscilla and the girls in his mother's care, they did not realise that he would be gone for the next eighteen months, travelling the length and breadth of the USA. Many of the students who heard him speak, had heard of the revival that had taken place in universities he had spoken at in Scotland and England, and had longed for something similar in their midst. As they listened to CT, they were challenged by his call to mission and committed themselves to serve in foreign missions. Hundreds answered the call. Some days CT would speak up to six times a day, and seldom for less than an hour if they allowed him. The passion for Christ and His service, that had been evident in the UK in student bodies, was equalled in America. When he was not speaking at meetings, CT was spending time with the Lord, or having one-to-one meetings with students to talk about their souls.

In a letter dated 14 January 1897, written from Minneapolis, he wrote:

> After tea had meeting from 7.30 to 8.30 pm. The Lord
> blessed the students and some others … that night young
> A. asked me to go for a walk with him; we talked over
> his case and he decided on a full surrender, which he
> completed in my room that night – a grand time.

In another letter dated 24 June 1897 from Knoxville he wrote:

> I have had such a good day today, early up and a Quiet
> Time for most of the day and the Lord has been opening
> up the Word. I always seem to get so lazy when I go home.
> Do pray for me. I find I do not understand the Word
> unless I spend much time with Him and then He makes
> the pages to shine. I am generally awake and reading and
> praying after 4 am.

Monmouth, 13 November 1897, he wrote:

> After tea the leader of the YMCA came and made a
> full surrender, asking for the gift of the Holy Spirit and

went away knowing that he had received, so bright and believing, and set on doing personal soul saving work.[8]

And so the letters back home to his wife and family go on. Every one of them speak of the blessing and response that CT had to the words he spoke – whether in a big meeting or one-to-one in his room.

When CT returned to England in April 1898, it was not to a wife and children who felt as blessed as him. Priscilla was ill and depressed. CT and Priscilla had definite ideas about how to raise their children but, with CT in the USA, Priscilla had found herself in a constant battle with a strong mother-in-law and a nanny and nursemaid, who thought they knew best how the children should be raised. Before returning to the UK, the children had been raised in a China where materialism was non-existent. Now they were living in a very wealthy household with rich cousins all around them. Life was not easy for them, or their parents.

Call of India

CT knew that one of the dying wishes of his father had been that he would one day have an opportunity to share the gospel with the Indian people. His father had told him that the people of northern India knew the name of Studd, but only as 'Studd the indigo planter, Studd the wealth seeker.' Now he wanted them to meet 'Studd the ambassador of Jesus Christ.' It was the land that his father had made his fortune, and now he wanted them to know of the God who changed his life.

Mr Vincent, his father's old friend, who had been the one who took Edward Studd to first hear D L Moody speak, urged CT to go to India. He even offered to make all the arrangements for him and to pay for the passage. In 1900 CT took up the challenge and sailed for India. He travelled extensively around the area where his father had had his plantations, preaching the gospel.

After six months of travelling, a church in southern India contacted him to ask if he would consider becoming their minister. The church in question operated under the auspices of the Anglo-Indian Evangelisation Society. It was an English-speaking independent Union Church based at Ootacamund, in southern India. CT was reluctant to give up his itinerant ministry, so the church agreed for him to spend two thirds of his time there and one third visiting English people in southern India. The position paid him a salary and gave him a home. CT accepted and asked Priscilla and the family to join him. He was to remain there until 1906.

The children and Priscilla (plus a governess, paid by CT's mother) arrived in Ooty in October 1900. Grace was nearly twelve years old and the youngest child, Pauline, was six. Life was not as demanding in India as it had been in China and CT was able to enjoy more time with his wife and children. It was also a cooler climate. Ooty, as the locals referred to it, was 7,500 feet above sea level, with a climate more like a good English summer.

CT immediately set to work making relationships and speak of his Lord wherever and to whomever he could. One such couple was the Governor of Madras and his wife, Lord and Lady Ampthill. Lord Amphtill was an old Etonian and so had a common link with CT and often invited him to the Governor's House.

On one occasion when CT's asthma was particularly bad, the Governor invited him and Priscilla to stay at the Governor's House and even arranged for their own doctor to perform a special nose operation on CT. Whilst there, Lord Kitchener was also in town. When introduced to CT, he is reported to have said: 'Ah, yes, of course, we all know Charles Studd!'[9]

The Studds' home was a real hub of activity. Somehow any visitors who came to the area ended up at the Studds' on a Sunday evening. The company was good and the conversation stimulating. But CT always managed to turn things towards the gospel. Wherever he was, reaching souls was CT's heart. Throughout his time in India, he saw conversions every week of both British and European expatriates, as well as local villagers. He, and his church, became known as 'the place to avoid unless a man means to get converted.'[10]

An example of one such conversion was that of a clerk in the Military offices. His son persuaded him to go to the Ooty Church. He went, and started being a regular attendee. There came the day when he wrote to CT:

Each Sunday at the Union Church I get hit harder and harder. This last week I felt I had to make my decision. There was a big fight between God and me and the devil. Thank God. He won.

The clerk's 'native boy' found the change so marked, the he wanted to know:

What has happened to my master? He (was) always talking plenty swear words: now he only doing plenty Church work.[11]

CT's cricketing prowess continued to open doors and he was invited to join a cricket tour. As this involved playing army regimental teams, he accepted the invitation because it gave him the opportunity of nightly meeting with the soldiers and discussing Christ with them. Fortunately, he had lost none of his old cricket skills. During 1904 he made two double centuries, which had only been achieved once before in Indian cricket!

However, despite his active life for his Lord, he was suffering very poor health. His asthma was a constant struggle and on some nights he could not go to bed but had to sit in his chair fighting for breath. In one of Priscilla's letters home, she wrote: 'Charlie is a wreck ... puffing and wheezing wherever he goes, and almost the slightest movement brings on asthma.'[12]

Ooty, however, proved to be a time of real happiness for the family. For the first and only time in his life, CT spent time imputing into the girls' lives. He taught each of the girls how to ride, play polo, tennis and even cricket.

In 1906, before the Studds left India to return to the UK, the four girls, who had made their own decision to follow Christ, expressed a desire to be baptised. The Studds were never conventional and the children's baptism was one example of this.

Much to the wider Studd family's disappointment, years earlier CT had left the Anglican Church and refused to have his children baptised as babies. Now the girls were aged between twelve and eighteen. It was decided that CT would baptise them but when and how? There was no church building with a baptismal pool for them to use and no nearby coast or lake of water.

CT asked his gardener to dig a large hole in their garden. He managed to purchase the biggest zinc-lined case he could find and fitted it into the hole. The weather was cold but CT arranged for young boys to carry kettles and saucepans, full of hot water, to fill the case. It took longer than expected because the case developed a leak!

Many from the local community came to watch. Amongst those present were the missionary Amy Carmichael, local church leaders and even the local vicar. The congregation sang; they prayed and CT invited someone in the crowd to ask each girl any questions they wanted about their faith. When they had answered, each girl went to the hole in the garden, entered the water and was baptised, as the crowd sang praises to God. With the baptismal service over, they returned to their house and had the most wonderful Lord's Supper together.

Later that same year, ill health again forced the family to return to the United Kingdom. The damp cool climate that was attractive to so many people, was not good for CT's asthma.

As they boarded a steamer bound for England, Priscilla was not to know that she would never again return to service on the mission field.

CHAPTER NINE

The Call of Africa

Cannibals Want Missionaries

Once back in the UK the family settled into their grandmother's house in Hyde Park Gardens.

Grandmother Studd was a sprightly seventy-two-year-old, who loved to have her family around her and showered love on the girls. Similarly, the girls loved being at their grandmother's. She knew how to love them in a way that CT and Priscilla never could. If the girls had a problem, it was likely to be the grandmother they would go and talk it over with. Not that they had long to do it.

Soon after returning to the UK the three eldest girls, Grace, Edith and Dorothy, went to boarding school in Switzerland. This was paid for by CT's sister, Dora, who was married to Willie Bradshaw, and it was hoped that, whilst they were there, they would learn French.

After eighteen months in Switzerland, the girls persuaded their parents to allow them to return to England. Sherborne School for girls in Dorset had been founded a few years before in 1899. It was considered the finest girls' school in the country. Again CT's sister, Dora and her husband, agreed to pay the fees so the girls could enrol there to finish their schooling.

As news of CT being back in the UK became known, he began receiving invitations to speak from all over the country. He was not one to sit and do nothing, and even asthma and other ailments were not going to stop him. He was still well-known across the UK for his cricketing exploits as well as the amazing meetings around the universities and conference halls. He accepted as many invitations as he could.

It is estimated that, between 1906 and 1908, he addressed tens of thousands of people, mainly men, and many with no religious conviction but who were drawn by his sporting reputation. CT's speaking ability had increased over the years and now he could address meetings in the language of the people, with humour and in a way that made men feel that he was speaking straight to them, man to man.

His directness became legendary. In one talk at a business lunch he addressed his audience by saying:

> You've had a rich dinner, I shall not tickle you with an
> academic display of language. I once had another religion:
> mincing, lisping, hunting the Bible for hidden truths, but no
> obedience, no sacrifice. Then the real thing came before me
> … Words became deeds. The commands of Christ became
> battle calls to be obeyed, unless one would lose one's self-
> respect and manhood. Instead of saying 'Lord, Lord' and yet
> remaining deaf to the simplest commandments, I began to
> rely upon God as a real father...[1]

One of Birmingham's daily newspapers reported on one meeting he spoke at, in Handsworth:

> Mr Studd is a missionary to emulate. And so all that band of college men from Handsworth thought, as they cheered him to the echo, this man with a red tie and slim athlete body and the young face. After more than twenty years of harness he is bubbling over with life and humour; no pessimism about him, no luke-warmness; he loves and he follows, he teaches what he believes, he keeps a brave sunshiny face through all. No subtleties appear to puzzle him; his faith is as brave, as his speech is clear and straight.[2]

CT never missed the opportunity to speak with a person about their soul. On one occasion he was staying with a good friend, Dr A T Wilkinson in Manchester. The doctor ordered a growler[3] to take him to the station, and told the cabby his fare was C T Studd, the cricketer. The cabby immediately began to chat about how he had watched CT play cricket at the Old Trafford Cricket ground. When this was told to CT, he got out of the cab and went and sat next to the cabbie, to talk with him about submitting his life to Christ.

The truth was dawning on CT that he could not travel everywhere, however much he wanted to! He therefore tried his hand at putting his thoughts in print. He compiled a booklet challenging Christians not to melt like chocolate, when the going got hot! He called it *The Chocolate Soldier,* and it became an instant printing sensation. In it he wrote:

> We should go crusading for Christ. We have the men, the means and the ways, for steam and electricity and iron

have levelled the lands and bridled the seas. The doors of
the world have been opened wide to us by God. We pray
and preach; we bow the knee, we administer the Holy
Communion ... we shout 'onward Christian solders,
marching on to war', and then ... and then? We whisper,
I pray thee have me excused!

What glorious humbug we are!

Five hundred million heathen have not yet been
reached ....[4]

CT could not keep still, but the gloom of the UK church depressed
him. He was approaching fifty years old and his body was racked
by years of being pushed. How long could he keep going? His
mind was drawn to return to India and maybe returning to a part
of the country where the climate would be better for his asthma.

That was until, in 1908, he was in Liverpool. As the forty-
eight-year-old CT walked down one of the main Liverpool streets,
he saw a sign. It stated: 'Cannibals want Missionaries!'

The sign had been put up by a German missionary, Dr Karl
Kumm, who had founded the Sudan United Mission, to advertise
his meetings describing his experiences travelling across Africa. CT
decided to go and listen to Dr Karl.

In central Africa many tribes had never heard of Jesus
Christ. Explorers, big-game hunters, Arabs, traders,
European officials, and scientists had all been to those
regions, but no Christian had ever brought the gospel ...
my friends we have to go soon.

The shame sank deep into CT's soul.

'Why have no Christians gone,' he pondered?

'Why don't you go,' God replied?

130

'The doctors won't permit it,' Studd answered.

God's voice came again: 'Am I not the Good Physician? Can I not take you through? Can I not keep you there?'[5]

It was one thing to sense the call, but he was forty-eight and had been in poor health for fifteen years. Practically, how could he face tropical Africa which was known at the time as the 'White Man's grave?'

He met and talked with Karl Kumm. Together they agreed to travel across Africa from Forcados in Southern Nigeria to Khartoum in Sudan. Ill-health was not going to stop CT. His family tried to talk him out of the idea but, despite tears from his mother and wife, he pressed on with the idea. As their daughter Edith described it: 'It sent my grandmother crying and my mother weeping silently on the third floor of Hyde Park Gardens.'[6] However, Priscilla's helpless cries of 'Oh, Charlie how could you?' were of no avail.

CT set about speaking everywhere he could in order to collect recruits. No offer of speaking did he turn down ... he slept anywhere.

However his body had other ideas. When it came time to leave with Karl Kumm, he was in bed with malaria and a raging fever and not able to go. CT was devastated but his wife and children rejoiced that their prayers had been answered.

Africa Beckons

In 1910 CT was booked to speak at the World Missionary Conference being held in Edinburgh, Scotland. As he sat and listened to other speakers, he could not help being challenged. One of the speakers present was Karl Kumm, who had now returned from his travels through Africa. He told the Conference:

> There are twenty-six separate tribes who have not been evangelised yet. They range in size from five thousand members to two million. These tribes, which are along the borders of central Africa, stand in the way of the advance of Islam. It will be to our eternal shame if, for want of a Christian missionary, these people are converted to Islam.[7]

Another of the Conference speakers was John Mott from the USA, who had been awakened to the call of the mission field, all those years previously by CT's brother Kynaston. CT was particularly challenged by one of John Mott's messages: 'Carrying the Gospel to All the Non-Christian nations.'[8] CT felt the call! He longed to go to Africa to explore the situation in southern Sudan for himself.

Out of the Conference a group of businessmen came together to arrange finance for those who sensed the call of God to reach the unreached tribes. The group agreed to pay CT's costs if he went to Africa. But they had a condition – that he had to receive doctor's approval to travel. CT immediately booked to sail on a ship departing from Liverpool's port for Africa.

However, arranging for the medical examination took a while longer and was something he put off doing. When he did, unfortunately the report was not good. The businessmen therefore felt they had no option but to withdraw their support for CT's travel. CT's response was characteristic:

> Gentlemen, God has called me to go and I will go. I
> will blaze the trail, though my grave may only become a
> stepping stone that younger men may follow. Jesus tells us,

'he that shall lose his life for my sake and the gospel's, shall find it, and if I lose my life following Jesus, so be it.[9]

He therefore sought to raise funds elsewhere but none were forthcoming. Even when he applied to join a number of missionary boards to go to Africa under their auspices, none would accept him because of his health issues. His medical doctor told him in no uncertain terms that it was too risky for him to go with all the health risks associated with equatorial Africa.

With no money to pay for his boat ticket, and his expenses once he was there, he was in a dilemma what to do. However, he told no one that the businessmen had withdrawn their support.

CT had made it a principle of his life that he never took up an offering or asked for money. Three weeks before the supposed departure day for Africa still he did not have the money. However, he was speaking the next day at a meeting in Birmingham. The Chairman, Dr J H Jowett, told the audience that CT was sailing for Africa in a couple of weeks. Sitting listening to the Chairman's remarks, CT wondered what to say, for he had not a penny piece! Then the light broke.

> A voice said to him in his heart: 'Are you going to the heart of Africa?'
>
> 'How can I, Lord, without the money?'
>
> 'Haven't you yet learned that when I give a commission, I give the provision also?'
>
> It was like the sun shining through the clouds, and CT got up and spoke as one about to sail.[10]

Next day, at a meeting at the Linacre Mission in Liverpool, someone pressed a £10 note into his hands. He took it as a sign he should still go. He used the money to go to the Bibby Line offices and confirm his ticket. There was the deposit. The rest would follow … and it did, through a gift of £300 from a business man in Cardiff. He now had enough to pay for his boat ticket to Africa.

On a cold, dull December day, *SS Warwickshire* sailed from Liverpool for Port Said, Egypt. CT was on board with the intention of making an exploratory trip to Khartoum in Sudan.

First Visit to Africa

As CT sat in his cabin on the 15 December 1910, his vulnerability was very real. He had a stubborn streak about him, but he also felt very alone. Here he was sailing from Liverpool to Africa. How could one person, a sick one at that, do anything in such a vast continent? He was certain that God was calling him to go to Africa, so despite opposition – even that of his wife who knew that she was not well enough to go with him – he sailed. As the ship began its voyage, he sensed God speak to him: 'This trip is not merely for Sudan. It is for the whole evangelised world.' It seemed a crazy notion but CT was a dreamer. He was reminded of the Scripture: 'Every place your foot shall tread upon I will give you' (Joshua 1:3). Writing to a friend he said: 'Thank God I have big feet!'[11]

To CT, faith in Jesus laughed at impossibilities. To his good friend Dr Wilkinson, he shared his heart: 'My soul is on fire to do the work of Christ. I seem to hear Jesus saying 'Go over and possess the good land of the world'.'[12]

Five days out at sea he wrote to Priscilla.

And now Scilla darling, all this separation is for our good, and what is better, it is for God's glory and Christ's honour. I believe this assuredly.

1. Your health shall be restored.

2. You shall become a bigger firebrand for Jesus than ever you have been, and a far greater power than poor weak I could ever be.

3. Our girls shall be white-hot Christian warriors and to God be all the glory.

I think and think and think, and all upon the same line – new Crusade. Things simply surge through my mind and head, and God speaks to me every time I lie down, and assures me that he is going to do a wonderful work.

Darling Scilla, you remember Shanghai? Well those days are going to occur again, only on a magnificent scale.[13]

As the *SS Warwickshire* approached the Africa coast, CT wrote again to his wife:

Let us in our old age re-consecrate ourselves to Jesus. He has done so much for us … he has kept us going, and kept our girls, and saved them. God grant that, as a silver wedding present, He may give us this noble work to do for Him in Africa … Seldom in a life do two people have the opportunity to forsake all twice, but we are being offered this privilege. Let us grasp it with both hands. [14]

The *SS Warwickshire* reached Mombasa, Kenya, where CT alighted and from where he made his way to Nairobi. The German missionary, Karl Kumm, had given him a letter of introduction to a Christian couple there who kindly allowed him to stay in their house for six weeks. Here he used the time to glean as much information as he could about Sudan and what Christian missions where doing to evangelise there. From Nairobi he travelled on to Khartoum.

Once he reached the capital of Sudan, he had time on his hands. CT was invited to speak at the English-speaking church by Bishop Gwynne of the Church Mission Society. He held a mission amongst the men of the Battalion of Northumberland Fusiliers who were stationed in Khartoum. He was also invited by Sir Reginald Wingate to dine at the Palace and share about his plans for missionary work. On one occasion he sat next to a lady, Mrs Wherry, who told him:

> I was at the Cambridge v Australia match at Fenners
> cricket ground in Cambridge in 1882 when you played
> and beat them. You made the winning hit to the boundary
> where I was sitting. The ball rolled under my petticoat.
> I stooped down, picked it up and threw it back. I have
> regretted it ever since. I ought to have kept it …. [15].

But CT was not there to reminisce about cricket. He was burdened to share Christ with as many as possible. Eventually the permissions came through for him to move on from Khartoum and explore the southern Sudan. He was accompanied by Bishop Gwynne and Archdeacon Shaw of the Church Missionary Society, along with ten porters and twenty-nine donkeys laden with provisions for the trip. Their plan was to spend two and a half months, undertaking a nine-hundred-mile trek through the Bahr-el-Chazal region[16].

As they set out, their progress was slower than anticipated. The fact it was the rainy season didn't help. The more they travelled, the more CT was convinced this was not the region he was meant to be working in. The Church Missionary Society was already

CT's mother and father, Edward and Dora Studd.

Cambridge Graduates 1879.

Left: C T Studd in cricket bat pose. © *WEC International*

Below: Evangelist Dwight Moody (1837-1899) who greatly influenced the Studd family.

English Cricket team winning Ashes 1883 *(top row, from left)*: William Barnes, Frederick Morley, Charles T Studd, George Vernon, Charles Leslie *(centre)*: George Studd, Edward Tylecote, Ivo Bligh (captain), Allan Steel, Walter Read *(front)*: Richard Barlow, Willie Bates. © *WEC International*

Left: George Müller (1805-1898) set up an orphanage in Bristol. He greatly impacted CT's life.

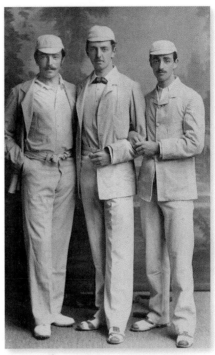

Right: The Studd brothers: Kynaston *(left)*, CT *(centre)* and George *(right)*.

© WEC International

The Studd's family home, Tedworth House, Wiltshire.

Top left: Young CT in Australia, c 1880. © *WEC International*

Top right: The Cambridge Seven *(clockwise from top)*: C T Studd, William Cassels, Arthur Polhill-Turner, Monty Beauchamp, Cecil Polhill-Turner, Dixon Hoste, *(centre)* Stanley Smith. © *WEC International*

Below left: Hudson Taylor (1832-1905), founder and leader of China Inland Mission.

Below right: Priscilla Studd.

Stanley Smith and C T Studd with their families in Chinese dress.

GRACE

DOROTHY

PAULINE

EDITH

CT and Priscilla Studd's four daughters.

Above: CT and Priscilla
Studd with family and
friends in India c 1903.
© *WEC International*

Right: A pensive C T
Studd. © *WEC International*

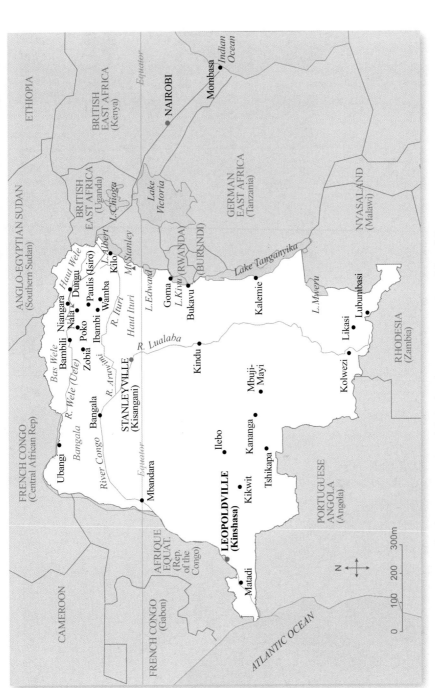

Map of Belgian Congo (c1940) (today the Democratic Republic of Congo). © *WEC International*

Right: Congo boys with
bow and arrow.

Below: Congolese chief,
wife and troops.

Left: Heart of Africa Mission Station (Nangara, Belgian Congo).

© WEC International

Right: CT surrounded by books in his tent home in the Belgian Congo.

Left: CT and fellow missionary Jack Harrison by tent. *© WEC International*

CT and others inspecting supplies. © *WEC International*

CT at his writing desk in Ibambi. © *WEC International*

Left: CT with his daughter Edith (Buxton). © *WEC International*

Right: Edith (CT and Priscilla's daughter) and Alfred Buxton with pygmy woman in the Congo, 1918. © *WEC International*

Below: CT and Alfred Buxton with colleague. © *WEC International*

Makutanu seated outside in Ibambi (A 'makutanu' was a special gathering of believers that met for several days for teaching and fellowship.) © *WEC International*

New missionary arrivals by canoe. © *WEC International*

Top: Wedding of Pauline Studd to Norman Grubb, 24 November 1919 (top row from left) Alfred Buxton, Revd Gilbert Barclay, Pauline Grubb (née Studd), Norman Grubb, Lt Col David Munro (bottom row) Edith Buxton and Susan, Ann Barclay, Dorothy Barclay (née Studd) and Mary, Priscilla Studd, Charles Barclay and Grace Munro (née Studd). © *WEC International*

Bottom left: A wistful Priscilla. © *WEC International*

Bottom right: C T Studd, later in life.

Left: C T Studd
surrounded by
WEC staff.

© *WEC International*

Right: C T Studd
with banjo, with
violinist and choir
in the Congo, 1929.

Left: The Belgian
Congo c 1900

Priscilla Studd arrives in the Congo, 1928. © *WEC International*

Priscilla Studd's visit to the Congo in 1928. (Note the DCD symbol on the car.)

© *WEC International*

Transporting Priscilla Studd's car on the river ferry during her 1928 visit to the Congo. © *WEC International*

The graves of C T Studd and fellow mission leader, Jack Harrison, at Ibambi (restored 2013). © *WEC International*

working well in the area. CT therefore decided that there was little point starting a new work. He did wonder whether he was meant to join forces with the Church Missionary Society but decided he could not work with Anglicans to reach the cannibals from the north![17]

As they travelled, CT kept hearing about a mass of people to the south of Sudan, in an area called the Belgian Congo. He understood that in this land there was no Christian witness and the name of Christ had never been preached. He believed that was where his destiny lay.

After ten difficult weeks, the party trudged back into Khartoum. Some of the porters had disappeared on the way, and twenty-five out of the twenty-nine donkeys they had started with, had died. However, CT's health had stayed well throughout the trip. He took that as a sign that God was in the trip and in his plans to start a new work in the Congo area. Unfortunately, however, within days of his return to Khartoum CT went down with a very bad attack of malaria. It was eight weeks before he recovered sufficiently to be able to travel back to the UK, fired up for a new Crusade in the Belgian Congo. He had been away for six months.

Launch of the Heart of Africa mission

A sick and weak CT arrived back in the UK from Africa and his recovery took most of the summer of 1911. As he lay on his bed, or rested on his couch, his mind was working overtime. He was trying to work out all he believed the Lord had revealed to him. It seemed crazy for one person – and a sick one at that – to dream such dreams. But he trusted his God.

CT therefore jotted down thoughts as they came ... a different kind of mission ... one for men and women with no thoughts for their own safety ... not linked to any existing denomination ... starting in central Africa, but unto the uttermost parts of the world.

As he worked, he began to firm up his ideas, scribbling down thoughts of what he wanted to bring into being. He gave it the name of the 'Heart of Africa Mission'. CT clearly hoped that others would become part of it, but decided that, to do so, they had to agree to certain conditions. He called the theological basis of the new work, *The Five Smooth Stones*, after David's encounter with Goliath in 1 Samuel 17.40, where he took with him five stones. The Five Stones were:

1. Absolute faith in the deity of each person of the Trinity.

2. Absolute faith in the full inspiration of the Old and New Testament Scriptures.

3. Vow to preach none other save Jesus Christ and Him crucified.

4. Obedience to Christ's command to love all who love the Lord Jesus sincerely, without respect of persons, and to love all men.

5. Absolute faith in the will, power and providence of God to meet every need in His service.[18]

All funding for the Mission was to be from God. Nobody was to be asked for a donation; no collections were to be taken at any meeting held in connection with the Mission.

Before finalising his plans for a new mission, CT made a

further attempt to find an organisation he could join. Years later, the African Inland Mission were going through their archives and found in their basement the application that CT made to them in November 1912. His answers on the application form were not quite what the society expected. When they asked the name of his pastor, he wrote: 'The Lord Jesus Christ,' and for information on the Church he attended, he replied 'His Church.' Even so, they accepted him!

Once he felt sufficiently recovered, CT began to accept some of the many invitations he received to speak around the country. The crowds were still eager to listen to him. As ever, his longing as he spoke was that others would be stirred for mission and reaching the lost. 'Christ wants, not nibblers of the possible, but grabbers of the impossible,'[19] was one of his favourite expressions

An American evangelist Dr R A Torrey was conducting a three-week mission at the Guildhall, at Cambridge University. CT was invited to speak as part of it and the first recruits to join him in his ventures into Africa came through that meeting.

As a result of all CT's speaking engagements, a total of twenty-four young men volunteered to go to the Belgian Congo.

New Home and New Headquarters

The Lord had given CT a wife and lovely girls but all their time, whilst in the UK, was spent staying at his mother's home. CT was finding this created a huge tension within himself, between his commitment to the Lord and his responsibilities to his family. Furthermore, his wider family expressed their disapproval for his constant travelling, believing it was causing much of his ill-health and accusing him of not looking after his family properly.

CT could see that Priscilla was seriously ill. She suffered constantly from asthma and a heart problem and never rose before midday. She was now never well enough to attend any meetings with CT and she longed for him to stay at home more, and for them to spend time together.

The children had their own struggles. However hard they tried, they knew their parents were sold out for the gospel and that they themselves were never high up in their list of priorities. Being a child of a missionary is never easy. Being a child, with a father like C T Studd, and the fame and aura that was around him, made it very difficult for his girls.

CT was to comment that the girls in face, figure, and every other way, took after their mother. Their formative years had been spent in China and then India. They were raised in an atmosphere of trusting in God for everything and being careful with all that they had. CT and Priscilla had given all their wealth away and trusted in God for their money. Yet, once they arrived in England, the girls mixed with the wider Studd family, who were one of the wealthiest families in the UK. Life was not easy for any of them.

Because of the society they were mixing with, the Studd girls were invited to events such as coming-out parties and similar society occasions. But what to wear at such events? They only had one 'posh' hat between them and as they attended the coming-out parties of their friends, they had to pass the hat around!

Grace was the eldest child, having been born in 1889. To escape the confines of Studd family life, she married a wealthy older man, Martin John Sutton. Unfortunately it was not a happy marriage and only lasted a few years before her husband's death on 14 December 1913. She then went on to become a nurse during the First World War. It was whilst nursing in Brighton that she met a brilliant soldier, David C D Munro who, in time was to become Lieutenant Colonel in the Gordon Highlanders. At this stage he had no faith in a living God. Even so they married on 20 November 1917. Years later, and after retirement from the army and a spell farming in Rhodesia (now Zimbabwe), they returned to London and David Munro surrendered his life to Christ.

Edith and Pauline both committed themselves to mission work and ended up on the mission field serving under their father. Dorothy, however, remained in the UK, working alongside her husband who was appointed Home Overseer of the mission. Somehow CT could never show his real feelings to any of his daughters and they always felt he was cold towards them.

As CT began his plans to return to Africa in 1913, resistance came from within the family. Priscilla knew that she could not accompany him but she did not want to remain living with her mother-in-law indefinitely.

Gradually CT became aware of the dilemma Priscilla was facing and he became convinced they should buy their own place in London. It would be a family home whilst he was away in Africa and a place he could return to when required. It became an obsession with him. In time he found a property, which he described as modest, adequate and, most important of all, a bargain. Its address was 17 Highland Road, Norwood, London. Estate agents would have described it as 'a large semi-detached six-bedroom house with a basement and fair-sized garden.'

CT described the house in this way:

As I was going to leave the country, and my family were going to stay at home, it was necessary to provide for them, at least a roof over their heads. I saw a house that looked the very thing, and at a wonderfully reasonable price ... I never dreamed of the future that was to be, but I felt I had to have that house, and it became such an obsession that at last my wife said to me, 'Oh, never mind the house; you don't get any sleep these nights thinking and praying about that old house. You go along and we will manage somehow.'

But it could not be done. In His usual way God provided for that house ... Little did I dream that that house was to be the headquarters of a mission of which I had never dreamed, but which evidently God knew all about. It turned out to be the headquarters of our new mission, and my wife became its presiding genius.[20]

For the first time in his life CT borrowed some money so he could buy it. It was going to cost all of £200 and a friend agreed to loan him the money. Priscilla was overjoyed at the idea of them having their own home. When his mother discovered about the loan, she was furious with him. As far as she was concerned it had to be family who helped him. She took it upon herself to loan him the money for the house and for the necessary furniture. Before the loan could be repaid, his mother had turned it into a wonderful gift.

Even with his mother's money, they could not afford new furniture, so spent much time trawling through second-hand furniture shops.

One day whilst travelling down Westbourne Grove in London, CT saw some second-hand furniture outside a shop. He went to look at it. No one was around, so he wandered into the store where more furniture was stored. As he did so, he walked through a door and entered a large room, where an auction was taking place. He couldn't believe how little money the furniture was being sold for. Before he left the auction that day, he had bought a library chair, upholstered in Morocco and with walnut wood. It had cost him fifteen shillings. He went back to the auction the next week. Prices were similarly very low and he bought more furniture for very little money.

CT had told Priscilla that the house needed to be covered with lino, as carpet was too expensive. Attending an auction with Priscilla one day, he was studying the catalogue when his wife poked him in the ribs: 'CT, do you see what these carpets are going for?' However, CT said he wasn't interested in them and that lino was what they needed. However, Priscilla pointed out that carpet was going at a cheaper price than they could purchase any linoleum. Eventually, he was persuaded and they bought the next carpet very cheaply indeed.

On another day Charles went to an auction in a private house.

> One of the last things auctioned were the electric light
> fittings. Until then I had no thought of having electric
> light in the house, for electricity had not come to our road.
> But all those fittings went for thirty-two shillings, and I
> was the purchaser, and that thirty-two bobs' worth are
> the electric light fittings of No 17. Chairs, tables, beds,
> sideboard and even pictures all came from the same source,
> and all at the same fancy prices. This is the way our Father
> supplied the furniture.[21]

The night before CT departed on his second trip to Africa, with electric cable having been laid passed their house by the municipality, the electric lights were switched on for the first time in No 17.

Saying Goodbye

Once Priscilla and the girls were settled into their home in Highland Road, CT felt released to journey to Africa. He was doing so under the auspices of the Africa Inland Mission, and three of the twenty-four young men who had volunteered to serve in the Congo, were already there, at Mombasa, waiting for him to arrive.

CT was travelling with Alfred Buxton as his assistant and helper. They were considered an 'odd couple': CT was too old and sick for Africa; Alfred, at twenty-one years old, too young.

As CT prepared for departure yet again, it was hardest for those left behind. Alfred, who was journeying out with CT, had just the week before, become engaged to the Studd's daughter, Edith. Now he was leaving her to go to Africa with her father. She wondered when she would next see him.

Priscilla had her own battles with the separation. She hated the thought that, in just a few days, CT would depart. She knew neither how long he would be away, nor whether he would even survive the journey. But, as she spent time with the Lord, peace came.

> That night before he left, I sat by the fire and began to weep. I do not often weep but I wept sore that night. Then I thought this will never do. I shall be ill tomorrow, and unable to help anyone. Going up in the train that day to Waterloo (Station in London), I had been reading a book

in which there were two references, one was Psalm 34 and the other Daniel 3.29. I had decided in my first spare moments I would read those passages, so I opened my Bible. The very first words seemed almost to knock me down. The first verse was:

I will … It means determination. It means grit, courage.

I will bless … I will make the Lord happy. That was not to be attained by weeping.

I will bless the Lord at all times. Before I got to the end of that verse the tears were gone, and I got to the point where I could say, I will make the Lord happy now. Then I read on.

I sought the Lord and he heard me and delivered me from all my fears. Then towards the end it says …

He keepeth all his bones, not one of them is broken. I coupled this to Daniel 3.29. I just felt every fear was gone, all my fears, all my troubles, all that deft alone. [22]

Priscilla knew in that instant she could trust the Lord, even with the fear of malaria fever and poison arrows of the savages. She went to bed rejoicing. 'I just laughed the 'laugh of faith' that night.'

Rising from her knees, Priscilla put her thoughts in letter form to CT. Although he had not started his journey, when she finished the letter she posted it to Marseille in France, to await the ship's arrival there. She wanted to assure him, all would be well. 'I rose from my knees and wrote the experience to my husband and posted it to Marseilles, though he had not yet left this country.'[23]

CT's final night in his home before he and Alfred departed was 29 January 1913. During the evening a young man called round to wish him well on his travels. They talked for a few moments about what sacrifice meant. As CT talked, words came into his mind that became the watchword for the new work: 'If Jesus Christ be God and died for me, then no sacrifice can be too great for me to make for him.' Before he went to bed that night, CT wrote them in his journal.

Once they had said their goodbyes and the ship had started on its journey, CT wrote to Priscilla:

> Well my darling, God was good to keep us so busy last night. He knew I could not stand much and so he engineered us right through and gave the glory in our souls.
>
> I shall ever picture you running up with the camera. I longed, but dare not, say goodbye or kiss again. I dare not. The tears came as I thought of your tears … Now let us thank Him in anticipation not only with our lips but with our lives.
>
> You little dream of how I know that you pay the greatest price, only I dare not say it to you, but I admire you darling and shall ever do so and God will give us His hundredfold … Goodbye my darling Scilla. We began risking all for God and we will end as we began, loving each other utterly and only less than we love Jesus.[24]

A new adventure was about to start.

Africa for a Second Time

CT would be gone from the UK for two years.

Norman Grubb, in his biography writes: 'Career and fortune had early gone on the altar; now health and home and family life went also'.[25] His sickly wife and four daughters stayed in England.

To any who cared to listen CT declared: 'The Committee I work under is a conveniently small Committee, a very wealthy Committee, a wonderfully generous Committee, and is always sitting in session – the Committee of the Father, the Son and the Holy Ghost.'

But all was not good for CT and Alfred. Once their ship arrived in Mombasa, they headed off to meet the three young recruits who had gone ahead to wait for them. Having arrived early, the three men had used their time talking with Christians in the area and telling them about their plans. Everyone they had talked with had told them the plans were foolish and would not work. Those who knew CT told them his health would not hold up.

Within minutes of meeting up with CT and Alfred, the three young men told them they were having second thoughts! What they really meant was they had changed their minds about travelling into the interior with the two of them. CT pondered what to do. He had been so looking forward to the five of them venturing forth together – all under the banner of the Africa Inland Mission. Should he continue just with Alfred? He was even afraid that if Alfred spent much time with them, he too would be persuaded not to continue with him.

His relationship with the Africa Inland Mission had been shaky from the start. Within days of joining the mission, CT had been requesting changes to the Mission's constitution. These were refused by the Mission's Council. In the end CT decided he was going to press on regardless and that he would terminate his membership of the Mission. It is not recorded, but it seems it was a resignation the Mission were happy to accept.

CT quickly purchased supplies that Alfred and he would need for the first part of their journey. They bade their goodbyes to the three young men and departed for Nairobi, where they boarded a train heading west to Lake Victoria. The journey continued by steamer across the Lake, then another train, another steamer across another lake, before they had a final car ride to a small Church Missionary Society mission station in Uganda, at Masindi.

As there was no room for them in the Mission house, they were given permission to pitch their tent in the grounds and sleep there. The next morning CT was up early and raring to go on the next leg of their journey. However, he discovered Alfred was not even able to get out of bed. He had a high fever and for several days he lay there, weak and unable to move.

As they waited for Alfred to recover, a telegram reached them that had been forwarded from Mombasa. It was from Alfred's father. CT thought receiving a message from his father would help Alfred's recovery but sadly it had the opposite effect. Alfred's father was telling him that he was withdrawing permission for him to continue his journey with CT into the interior.

In his mind CT went over the events that had led to Alfred joining him in the first place. Alfred had obtained his Cambridge degree and was in the midst of a medical course, when he heard CT speak about the needs of Africa. He felt the call to go with him. Initially his father had been against it but, over time, he gave his approval. Alfred's father, the Rev Barclay F Buxton, had himself been a missionary in Japan, and was an old friend of CT's from his Cambridge days. Now this news. CT assumed that somehow Alfred's father had heard that the other three volunteers had withdrawn.

Rather than talking things over with Alfred, CT left him alone.

He sensed the right thing to do was to pray and to allow Alfred to reach his own decision.

Alfred had a real battle as he sought God's will for his life. When he next talked with CT, he told him he knew he must stay with him. His calling was from God and he must obey Him.

As CT questioned him about how he had reached his decision, he told him he had been meditating on Psalm 105:

> When they were but a few men in number; yea very few
> and strangers in it. When they went from one nation to
> another, from one kingdom to another people; he suffered
> no man to do them wrong: yeah, he reproved kings for
> their sakes; saying, 'Touch not mine anointed and do my
> prophets no harm' (Psalm 105:12-15).[26]

In time the fever left Alfred and, amazingly, during the next two years he never had even an hour's attack of fever after that.[27]

However, the enemy had not finished trying to stop the trip before it even started. Before they left their campsite, one of the porters helping to carry their equipment, was lighting a candle. A sudden gust of wind blew it in the direction of the tent. The canvas tent exploded into flames and all their equipment inside it was destroyed. They were just thankful that no one was injured. CT wondered whether to return to Mombasa for more equipment – but decided retreat was not an option. They must press forwarded.

As soon as Alfred felt well enough, they set off. After a three-day forest trek in a westerly direction, they arrived on the shores of Lake Albert, on the British side. In the distance they could see the hills of the Belgian Congo. People around them told them: 'The Belgians won't let you in'. You are British.' CT and Alfred knelt on the ground and asked God for his favour with Government officials, and the direction to enter the land.

The next day, they took the steamer across Lake Albert to Mahagi. All the way across the words: 'We need favour from the officials,' were on the lips of CT and Alfred.

And that is what they were given. The officials on the Belgium side welcomed them. They wished them well on their travels. CT and Alfred had brought bicycles with them. As they headed towards Kila a distance of some eighty miles, they sped ahead of the porters who were carrying what remained of their equipment.

Soon they were travelling through the hostile territory of the Balenda tribe. The porters were fearful of even being in the area. The tales of what the Balendas had done to previous travellers were legendary. One particular day, the speed of CT and Alfred on their bicycles, meant that they were far ahead of their porters. When they reached what appeared to be a fork in the path they were following, they went one way and should have gone the other way.

Soon the two of them were hopelessly lost in the dense African jungle. Worse still they were separated from their porters who were carrying all their food and supplies. As they searched for signs of the direction to go, they came to a clearing. They sensed that eyes were watching them. Out of the bush a man appeared wearing nothing but a ragged shirt. He came towards them. The one thing that CT noticed was that he was smiling … and his teeth had been filed to sharp points. A sure sign that he was a cannibal!

However, the man seemed to sense they were lost and indicated he meant them no harm. He beckoned them to follow him. They had no choice. After following him for about an hour they came to a clearing with a cluster of grass huts. A fire was lit and they were beckoned to sit at it. They wondered if it was a trap. People came out of the grass huts to stare and gaze at them. CT and Alfred couldn't help noticing the sharpened teeth. Their new friends cooked food on the fire and gave it to them to eat. The two travellers didn't care to ask what animal the meat was from! CT was to later say that he thought maybe they were not interested in Alfred and him, as both of them were lank, lean and tough.

The Lord preserved them. They parted the best of friends amidst considerable applause. When they stood up to leave CT wondered how to thank them. He had no money to give them – not that money would have meant anything to their new friends. All he had to offer were the bright buttons on his trousers. He tore a few off and gave them to the man who had first found them. He seemed well pleased.

The watching people smiled and applauded as CT and Alfred departed, going in the direction they pointed them in. The porters had realised CT and Alfred must have taken a wrong turning and were searching for them. Thankfully they met up and by nightfall were back on the right path. Four days later, on 5 June 1913, they reached Kilo, a gold mining centre.

Their entrance caused quite a stir. The people of the town lined the streets as two white men, balanced on strange contraptions with only two wheels, entered the town.

CT thought they were there for just a few days but it was to be a long uncomfortable three months. Post was waiting them in Kilo. One was a letter to tell CT he had become a grandfather for the first time. His daughter Dorothy and her husband, the

Rev Gilbert Barclay, had had a baby girl, who they were naming Ann. Another letter was from Alfred's father, apologising for his previous message, and telling him that Alfred's brother, George, was interested in joining them.

The hardest letter for CT to receive, was one informing him Priscilla was seriously ill and that her heart was failing. She had decided to attend the Keswick Convention, held each July in the Lake District. Having enjoyed the week, when the Convention finished, she had travelled to Carlisle to enjoy some time with their daughter Dorothy and their new grand-daughter.

Apparently whilst there Priscilla had become seriously ill. The doctor who examined her, told her she needed to prepare for death. Her heart was found to have extended by several inches. Stimulants were the only things that kept her alive. A dear friend of theirs, Lord Radstock, was also at the Keswick Convention. When he heard the news he immediately took the train to Carlisle to pray with Priscilla. Thankfully she did not die, but the doctors then told her she would be an invalid for the rest of her life and that she would need to retire to bed each day early and not get up until midday the following day.

Within the letter with the news of Priscilla, was a message to CT telling him he needed to come home urgently. As was his custom when asked to do something, he took it to the Lord in prayer.

CT's response was not quite what those in the UK expected. He wrote and said: 'I really believe God has us in tow, and that He intends to execute His work of evangelising the world. By God's grace I intend to be in the job for all I'm worth, come life or death, committee or no committee, helper or no helper.' He was not returning to the UK. Years later CT, writing about the summons to return home, simply said, 'God gave me a different order'.

Deepest Congo

The life of the two missionaries was very basic, but not easy. The wind, rain and storms attacked the tent they were living in. CT and Alfred had come expecting sunshine and heat. They had a bed, a box and a basin. Cooking was outside on a fire even when it rained. This often meant they were living in constantly wet clothes, sometimes for as long as a week.

When they were in Kilo their days took on a routine. They rose at 5 am and had separate Quiet Times with the Lord until 8 am. Alfred spent the mornings attempting to learn some basic local dialect language, whilst CT wrote tracts and articles to send to Priscilla. In the afternoon, CT had to have a nap. At the close of the day, after their evening meal, they would walk around the town and then retire to bed at 9.00 pm.

The African fever really attacked CT whilst they were in Kilo and he could not shake it off, gradually becoming weaker and weaker. He was reminded of the instruction in the book of James to call the elders, and anoint with oil and pray. There were no elders, only a twenty-one-year-old assistant. There was no oil, except for what was in the kerosene lamp. They would have to make do. So young Buxton, with his kerosene oil, anointed CT's forehead and the two of them prayed. CT went to bed sick, feeling as if death was near and woke up ... healed.

On 28 August 1913, they departed from Kilo on their bicycles, with porters behind, carrying their belongings. The conditions in the Ituri forest were treacherous – wet, dark, and they were constantly slipping. For food CT and Alfred mainly lived on bananas, bread and tea. Four days into the trek the porters gave up, downing the goods they were carrying and disappearing into the gloom of the forest. What now for CT and Alfred? The two of them could not carry all the equipment they had with them. Should they just abandon it?

After discussion, it was decided that CT would remain on his own with the belongings, and Alfred would make his way to the nearest Belgian government station and try to recruit some more porters. This he did. After some haggling over rates of pay, they had their new porters.

Onward they trekked to Arebi. It was mainly forest and hills with few people and fewer animals. The forest journey should have taken eleven days but the stoppage because of portage problems, made it much longer.

They continued their journey from Arebi to Dungu, and were even able to ride their bicycles some of the way, rather than carry them. Six weeks after leaving Kilo they arrived in Dungu. CT had thought Dungu would be where they would make their base, as he had been assured it was an un-evangelised area.

He was therefore shocked to discover that four members of the Africa Inland Mission had based themselves there, having arrived in Dungu only ten days previously. He was dumbfounded when he discovered that two of the four young men were Morris and Batstone, two of those who had been waiting for CT at Mombasa in Kenya, and then decided not to go with him. CT confronted them as to what had happened.

Sheepishly they explained that, having decided not to journey with CT, they had discovered the Africa Inland Mission had two men in Mombasa about to depart for the Congo, and they had decided to go with them. They had taken a different route to Alfred and CT and not had the same delays. Thus, although they had started after them, they had arrived before them.

CT had no intention of starting a competing work. He decided they had no choice but to move on. However, they needed a week in Dungu to regroup and get organised so a Belgian merchant offered them the use of his guest house and they gladly accepted. The first night they were in the house there was a fierce storm, which seemed directly overhead. The noise of the thunder and the flashes of lightning were terrifying. Suddenly there was an enormous crash. The guest house had been hit. Some plaster fell from the ceiling. As they raced outside to see what was happening, they saw the thatched roof of the house was on fire. Despite the fierce rain the flames took hold. CT and Alfred rushed back in to grab what they could of their belongings and raced back out.

A crowd had gathered to watch, including a tall white man wearing nothing but a towel around his waist. He introduced himself as Count Ferdinand de Hemricourt de Grunne, a young lieutenant officer and the Belgian Commissioner for the district. He offered them use of one of his properties whilst they stayed in Dungu.

Count de Grunne, as well as being the Commissioner, was also a member of the Roman Catholic Church and welcomed the work the missionaries were seeking to do. He gave them favour, much help for their onward trip, and concessions to work in the area. He advised them to travel on to Niangara, and gave them maps of the area.

After a week in Dungu, CT and Alfred moved on down the Uele River for three days in a canoe. On 16 October 1913, they landed at Niangara, which CT considered the very heart of Africa. The next few months were spent scouting out the region, seeking to know the right area for the Mission's base. Each time they came back to saying it should be at Niangara. They were not to know it at the time but the great tropical forest that Niangara was on the edge of, stretched for hundreds of miles and contained the largest population in the whole of the Congo – tribes known by the names of Bazande, Mangbetu, Medje, Budu and Pygmies.

CT and Alfred sensed their adventure was succeeding beyond their wildest dreams. They did not know how far the work would grow or which direction, but they believed they had found the place to put roots down. In the December they went in search of an area of ground to build a Mission station, which could be the headquarters. Each time they found somewhere, local natives objected and opposed them. They therefore widened the area they were looking in and went south to an area called Nala. Here they found an ideal site; the Chief of the area gave his consent and the land became theirs.

With government favour, especially that of Count de Grunne, they built a Mission station at Niangara and another at Nala. The Niangara station cost six pound and was named 'Buckingham Palace'. It was 75 feet in length and 35 feet wide with another shed for meetings. It was made of mud and wattle (a collection of interwoven sticks and twigs). After all the months living in tents, it seemed to them like a palace – hence the name they gave it.

At Nala they were offered an abandoned government post with brick buildings already built, that the local people did not use. The head man of Nala even offered them a tract of land on which CT believed a school and hospital could be built.

Just living in the Congo had challenges. One day the boy who cleaned CT's room ran to tell him that he (CT) had been sleeping the previous night with a thin green snake in his bed. Just one bite from it would have killed him. That day in his Bible reading, he was reminded of Psalm 91 and the promise of angels who did not sleep, and kept charge over him.

CT wrote to the Home Committee he had set up before leaving the UK, sharing news of their progress. He told them that they urgently needed a minimum of a doctor and a teacher to join them in the Congo. He addressed the letter to Martin Sutton, their eldest daughter Grace's husband, who was Chairman of the Committee. The postal service in the Belgian Congo was a once a week affair. As CT's letters were taken, other letters were delivered to him from the UK.

The week that the letter to Martin Sutton was sent, was the week that a letter arrived urging CT to return to the UK. Two of his strongest supporters – Lord Radstock and Grace's husband, Martin Sutton – had gone to be with the Lord. They had been such a rock to him and he had been so glad that they were standing with Priscilla on the home front. Now they had gone. CT's health really wasn't good, his body was struggling with the Congo heat and lifestyle and he was feeling very weak. If they were to make any further progress with the Mission, it had to be in the strength of the Lord.

Rather than depart back to the UK, CT believed God was calling them to extend the area they were working in. He therefore decided to move out from Nala to explore. They passed through an area where ten years previously the first white man had ventured with thirty-five soldiers. The white man had been told by the natives in the area to go no further or he would be killed. He took no notice and he and thirty-three of his soldiers were killed, cooked and eaten! Thankfully the natives were more welcoming to CT and Alfred. Excited children ran in front and behind them, shouting, laughing and helping them through streams and rivers, across ram-shackled bridges, and up and down deep ravines. They did not speak each other's language but somehow, they communicated.

People were everywhere. To CT he had reached his *El Dorado* – this was the land God had promised. Here were a people who had never heard of the living God. CT believed he should live (and if need be, die) to declare the glory of God to these people.

More treks followed. Journeying five days northwest of Nala they reached Poko, and after then another six days they reached Bambili. During their trip south, the Belgian Commissioner had granted them several large concessions for missions as far south as Wamba on the edge of the Ituri Forest. These were all strategic centres for the young Heart of Africa Mission that CT intended establishing in the area.

Unbeknown to any of them, as CT and Alfred were returning to Niangara from their Mission treks with renewed zeal for the opportunities before them, war was breaking out across Europe. A young man by the name of Gavrilo Princip had assassinated Archduke Franz Ferdinand of Austria on 28 June 1914. War commenced across Europe. Britain only became involved in the war because the King of England issued Germany with an ultimatum that Belgium should remain neutral. Germany ignored the order and promptly overran Belgium on their way to attacking France.

CT first learned about the outbreak of war on 19 August when an official telegram arrived announcing fighting between Russia, Serbia and Austria. Europe was a long way from Africa but it still had an effect on CT's work. The Belgian Congo (roughly 75 times the size of Belgium) was flanked on two sides by German colonies.[28] However, CT brushed aside any effect that the War in Europe might have on them: 'The war is just one more trial of faith, but we laugh at the idea of it hindering us … always advance … no retrenchment.'[29]

Very soon after, they noticed the majority of Belgian officers stationed at Niangara, had been called away to fight in what became known as the African Colonial War.

The First Baptisms

On 19 June 1914, a couple of weeks before the outbreak of war, the first baptismal service was held in Niangara. Twelve locals were baptised. It was a wonderful time as the baptismal candidates answered simple questions concerning their belief. Once baptised, everyone joined in singing: 'Oh t'was love'.

The only disruption to the service was the firing of a revolver into the water to scare away crocodiles who had decided to investigate what was going on.

Six months later Nala had its first baptismal service with eighteen locals going through the waters of baptism. They each carried a large stone from the stream to form a heap in the middle of the Mission station as a testament to their dedication to God.

CT sent news back to the UK of some of the testimonies from the baptismal candidates. Whilst Priscilla was keeping to the doctor's orders about staying in bed every morning, she used her bed as a desk and an office, forming prayer centres, writing monthly pamphlets to send out to new and existing supporters, producing the first Heart of Africa Mission magazine.

Rather than dying as the doctors thought might happen, Priscilla had decided she was going to join in the fray of the new Crusade as much as her husband. So it was that Priscilla circulated news of the testimonies from the baptismal services. The Salvation Army's paper *The War Cry* made much of them, under the headlines: 'Ex-cannibals, drunkards, thieves, murderers, adulterers and swearers enter the kingdom of God.'[30]

It was hard for those who read the testimonies to take it all in. Some of the stories had the missionaries scratching their heads as well. The stories were of killings, and the eating of the body parts once they had been stewed, along with many other gruesome details.

In one of the periodical mailing drops to CT and Alfred, news reached them of five young men on their way to join them. They were thrilled at the news, but it made CT realise that it was not five more workers they needed but a hundred and five or a thousand and five. He concluded that he needed to return to the UK and begin a massive recruitment campaign for workers for central Africa.

He and Alfred talked. They agreed that Alfred would stay to meet the five new workers. He would then take responsibility for developing the work in Nala, and seek to learn more of the local language. CT made arrangements to leave. He assured Alfred he would return as soon as possible with many more workers. The trek back to the UK meant for CT a journey of 300 miles to the Congo River, then canoeing 700 miles to the river mouth, hopefully there to meet up with a ship to take him back to England.

It was the end of 1914. He found a ship. CT was to write: 'The first vessel sunk by a (German) U-boat happened the night before the vessel I was on arrived in England.'[31]

CT had been away from the UK for almost two years. The work of the Heart of Africa Mission had been established in Africa, but the only person he had left in charge was a twenty-three-year-old rookie, who had matured beyond imagination during the two years he and CT had been together.

CHAPTER 10

England Again

CT's Return

Priscilla and the girls were so excited to see CT when he arrived back in England in January 1915. Of course, he too was delighted to be back with his family, but he again struggled to settle into the routine of English life. The high society that the wider Studd family revelled in, was no longer something that he enjoyed or even wanted to be part of. He was not comfortable sitting in fine chairs and eating 'proper meals' with tables laid with the best of cutlery and linen serviettes. The hardship of life in the Congo had changed him. All he wanted to do was to share his experiences with as wide an audience as possible, and then return to the Congo as soon as he could.

CT was to stay in England for eighteen months. He used the time to travel the length and breadth of the country with the same energy and verve that he had trekked in Africa. Sometimes as he preached, the malaria and fever attacked him. But nothing was going to stop him pleading the cause of reaching those who had never heard the good news of the Gospel. When on a speaking tour in north Wales in November 1915 he wrote:

> Hughes Jones, mine host (at Colwyn Bay), brought in a doctor to examine me, who forbade me to go out and speak that evening. He told me that I must go home at once. I laughed and spoke for an hour and a half; next day Caernarfon two hours; then Bangor three meetings, and then Aberystwyth. Oh those train journeys! So slow and so cold but God is always there.[1]

CT and F B Meyer at Keswick

In the early 1900s one of the most popular speakers at the annual Keswick Convention was pastor and Bible teacher, Frederick Brotherton Meyer, more commonly known by his initials, F B Meyer. When he died in 1929, the *Daily Telegraph* newspaper described him as 'the Archbishop of the Free Churches'. C T Studd had considerable influence upon his life as we have seen earlier when CT and Stanley Smith visited his church in Leicester in 1884, as part of the tour of the UK prior to the Cambridge Seven leaving for China.

In July 1915 CT had some free time in his diary so he decided to attend the Keswick Convention. He was sitting amongst the congregation in the big tent, waiting to listen to F B Meyer expound the Scriptures when, from the front of the meeting, he was asked to come up to the platform and give an impromptu fifteen-minute report on his work in Africa.

Slowly he made his way to the front and began to share stories of what God was doing in Africa. As he did so, the most amazing thing happened in the meeting – God came down. A sense of God's Spirit filled the place, and there was a brokenness on the gathered crowd, and people began to weep as he shared with them his experience of serving the Lord on that great continent.

When CT descended from the platform, Meyer didn't know what to do. He could hardly speak let alone preach. He found it difficult trying to follow what had happened. When the meeting was over, Meyer sought out CT. As they talked, Meyer was incredulous and wanted to know what CT had done. But, of course, it wasn't CT, it was God.

They spent time talking. Here was Meyer, a great expositor and preacher of the Word of God, this key note speaker at the Keswick Convention – and he was being ministered to by a broken missionary from Africa called Charles Studd.

'Have you given all of the keys of your life to Jesus Christ?' CT asked. 'Do you know what that means? Like the keys of your house, to every room. Have you given every compartment, every secret place to Jesus Christ, that He might fill it?'

Meyer realised that he had never done that, and so that evening, after the Convention was over for the day, he went alone with God and he began to give the keys over to Him. He gave the key of family. He gave the key of possessions. He gave the keys of his future and his health. He used Hebrews 12 as a key verse where it says: 'Lay aside every sin, and the weight that weighs us down, keeping us from running the race.'

Meyer found that there was one key in his life that was a real problem for him to lay down. This was his popularity as a preacher. It was his reputation as an expositor of the Word of God. He struggled to give it up. As he struggled in his spirit over reputation, he heard God's Spirit speak to him. God said to him: 'Everything or nothing! Partial obedience is disobedience.' Like Jacob, he wrestled with God and broke through. Once he had given up his reputation, God came and met him![2]

C T Studd and F B Meyer became great friends after that Keswick Convention. They referred to each other simply by their initials CT and FB. Once, when they were both speaking at the same Convention, they shared a tent with one another. On one of the mornings, very early, FB was woken up by CT on his knees with a candle lit and an open Bible, and he was weeping. Gently FB asked him: 'What is wrong, brother? What are you doing?' As the tears streamed down his cheeks, CT replied: 'The Lord spoke to me this morning as I was waking up, and He said "If you love Me, keep my commandments". There are so many that I have not obeyed! That was C T Studd! The reason for God's blessing on his life was that he walked with God.

> In his mission's *Heart of Africa* magazine he wrote:
> Christ's call is to feed the hungry, not the full; to save the lost, not the stiff-necked; not to call the scoffers but sinners to repentance; not to build and furnish comfortable chapels, churches and cathedrals at home ... but to raise living churches of souls among the destitute, to capture men from the devil's clutches and snatch them from the very jaws of hell, to enlist and train them for Jesus and make them into an Almighty army of God. But this can only be accompanied by a red-hot, unconventional unfettered Holy Ghost religion, where neither Church nor State, neither man nor traditions are worshipped or preached, but only Christ and Him crucified.[3]

It is interesting to note supporters' comments to what they read about the new mission. Priscilla shared at a meeting, one response she had received: 'We read your magazine with interest. You are humanly speaking one of the craziest missionary societies that ever existed; but if sanity means modernism and no souls saved, may God grant you may never be sane.' When Priscilla shared that comment, she ended by saying: 'and so say all of us.'[4]

News from Alfred in the Congo said it as it was. One letter reported that one of the five new missionaries who had arrived in the Congo, had died from a tropical disease. Another letter spoke of eighteen new converts who had been baptised. The testimonies that Alfred shared in the letters continued to make gruesome reading: 'My father killed a man and I helped to eat him .... I did witchcraft from the finger nails of a dead man, and with the medicine killed a man.'

The date rapidly approached for CT to return to the Congo. Returning with him were eight recruits. Included amongst the number was his daughter Edith, excited, yet scared, as she went to join her fiancé and be married to him in the Belgian jungle.

Departure date was set for 24 July 1916 from Paddington Station. A huge crowd gathered to see the band of missionaries depart. Priscilla was there, this time not only saying goodbye to her beloved husband, but to her daughter also. Promptly at 9.40 am, with steam billowing out of its engine, the train pulled away from the platform. Neither CT nor Priscilla realised that it would be the last time that CT would depart the UK. He would never return. Indeed apart from a few days when Priscilla visited the Congo, they would never meet again on earth.

Priscilla's Healing

Priscilla's health took a remarkable turn for the better the day after CT departed from the UK. The very next day the Lord touched her life and she became a different woman. ... CT described what happened to her as 'Mother's resurrection is the greatest miracle I know of'. In one letter CT described how the Lord had sent down a cyclone of blessings upon her: 'A cyclone hit my wife ... China.'

From being the invalid of the Mission who could never get out of bed until almost lunchtime, she became the mission's deputation secretary and the chief speaker at all the annual and other public meetings. In time, she travelled to Canada, Australia (including Tasmania) New Zealand, South Africa and Spain to promote the work. Her life became a whirlwind of activity. Wherever she was, she would speak at least twice a day when she was not travelling. She was known as a lady of great charm and exceedingly strong personality. She had no other thought than the salvation of souls and looking after her children.

When the General Secretary of WEC, Rev Hindle, wrote about Priscilla for the forward of a book on her life, in July 1930, he wrote:

> How she waded through all the correspondence that passed
> through the office is a mystery, especially in addition to the
> volumes of correspondence dealt with in her own home.
> She familiarized herself with the minutest details both of
> correspondence and finance; and her intimate knowledge
> of all associated with the mission, whether as subscribers,
> helpers, intercessors, candidates, etc., was truly wonderful,

and can only be accounted for by the fact that her whole being was devoted to the work[5].

On one occasion Priscilla was holding a very strenuous campaign in Ireland, extending over a month, to promote the Mission work. To attend the monthly committee meeting (in London) during such a campaign was very inconvenient to do, but Priscilla knew she could do both. Immediately after speaking at a meeting in Ireland, she took the night boat to Holyhead, travelled down to London for the committee meeting, which began at 12 noon; then did the journey in reverse, to continue her meetings in Ireland. Where did her strength and ability to handle all the business of a busy mission come from? Every morning at 9 am, she would join the staff and volunteers for the office prayers. It was always evident to the most casual observer that she had long been in an audience with the King before joining with the office staff. She knew she could only do what she did by spending time with her Lord.

Those who knew her said that there was not a finer missionary speaker in the country. She lived and breathed her husband's experiences in Africa, and shared them as though she had experienced them herself. Addressing one of the Annual meetings, the subject she spoke on was: 'Five packed minutes in a crazy Mission.'

They were a crazy mission but God was about to do amazing things with these crazy people! Nothing was too much trouble for her.

CHAPTER 11

The Congo Once More

The Congo's First European Wedding

CT's journey back to Africa with his new recruits was a hazardous one since German U-boats were prowling the waters. The ship had 'watchers' posted around the ship looking for the enemy. Apart from the brave missionaries, the only other passengers on the boat were Belgian officials on their way to take up posts in the Belgian Congo. The tension and fear they showed was palpable. Even so CT gathered his new recruits each morning to train them on what to expect in the Congo, for study on the Bangala language and, in the afternoons, for Bible study on the great heroes of the faith.

Thankfully no German U-boats found them, and the ship entered the comparative tranquillity of the mouth of the Congo River on 27 September 1916.

Once on the Congo River the journey was far from over.

The ship docked at Matadi and the missionaries had five days under canvas whilst they gathered supplies and waited for a train to take them the twelve-hour journey to Kinshasa. Then there was another steamer for the 200-mile journey up the Congo River. By now the new recruits were realising just how hot the tropics could be.

They alighted where the Congo River and the Uele River crossed. Alfred was waiting there to be reunited with his fiancé. What a reunion they had! How faithful Alfred had been in remaining in his task in the Congo for four years, and resisting the lure to return to England and claim his bride. Those who knew Edith described her as 'beautiful, vivacious and fond of fun.'[1]

That first evening the new recruits gathered around as Alfred shared news of what God was doing in the Belgian Congo. There were now sixty baptised Christian believers in Nala. Other villages were asking for missionaries to come and tell them about this Jesus who changed lives.

Some of his stories were breath-taking. One of the missionaries had encountered a new tribe. The natives had asked him if he was English. A strange question he had thought. When he said he was, they took him to see a member of the tribe who told him a story. 'Several years ago, when I was a teenager, I had a vivid dream. In the dream God spoke to me. 'Wait for the English, they will tell you about me.'

The tribe assumed 'English' meant a god-person and didn't know it was a nationality. Ever since the dream, the people of the village had questioned any white person who crossed their path, to find out if they were English.

Alfred told the new recruits that the Heart of Africa missionary had set them straight and introduce them to Jesus Christ.[2] The story about the English came out when a baptismal candidate, Jabori, shared his testimony. His story was so remarkable that the missionaries checked with others to verify what he said was true.

Jabori's story as he told it was:

> I was a great warrior. When the Belgians wanted a village
> or chief to be subdued, they would send for me. I became
> very ill and lost all consciousness and died. My friends had
> dug my grave and (were) putting me into it when I rose up
> and said I had seen God Himself, who had told me that
> before long the English would come and tell us all about
> the true God and truth. I told this vision to many … and
> because of this the people used to speak of God by the
> name of 'English'.[3]

A few days later they were on a smaller steamer travelling up the Uele River for another week, then by foot for 300 miles through forests. Their journey had taken them four months.

The Africans had heard the missionaries were coming and drums made sure everyone knew about their arrival. As they reached the outskirts of the area, groups of African Christians walked alongside them, singing hymns and reciting Bible verses. When CT had left the area, Christianity was sparse and not much established. Now it was so different. He found it hard to hold back the tears. On the outskirts of the village, cries of joy went up from the Christians, as they rushed to greet CT and the new missionaries. One of those cheering and welcoming him back was Sambo. He had been their first convert at Nala. Now he had walked a full day to be part of the welcoming group.

CT described it as like a Lord Mayor's show, with the crowds and their drums and bugles. A house had already been prepared for CT and the new recruits, which they immediately entered. They all stood on the steps and at the top of their voices sang the Doxology. Then they tucked into an enjoyable meal the people of Nala had prepared of pineapples, bananas, roast chicken, sweet potatoes and greens; all served on a rough-hewn table.[4]

God had greatly blessed the soul-winning efforts of Alfred and the missionaries who had served with him. Four Mission stations were established in an area inhabited by eight different tribes. The congregation at Nala, where Alfred was based, had grown to sixty members. What a change in the three years. In time it was to consist of forty houses, a blacksmith, a carpentry, a hospital, separate girls' and boys' schools and two leper camps.[5]

Once the party had settled in Nala, it was time for CT, with Alfred and his fiancé Edith, to trek for five days to Niangara for their wedding. Edith's arrival caused quite a stir. The Belgian Government had decreed that the Congo was not civilised enough for western women to live in, so no Belgian officials were allowed to bring their wives with them. Edith (and the two missionary ladies who had travelled with her) were the only known European women in the region.

On 16 December 1916 the missionary party gathered to celebrate two weddings! 'Buckingham Palace', the little Mission station built by CT and Alfred, was still there and that was the first wedding venue. It was crowded out with onlookers as CT led the service. Despite the heat and surroundings, Alfred and Edith looked beautiful. The service was followed by a tribal feast. Then, later the same day, in front of ten Belgian officials who wore full dress uniforms and medals, a twenty-minute legal ceremony was conducted by the District Commissioner. More refreshments followed the wedding and then it was time for Alfred and Edith to take their leave for a short honeymoon on a nearby island.

A Church Begins to Blossom

CT knew the region between African's longest river (the Nile) and Lake Chad was the largest un-evangelised area in Africa. He therefore knew he had a task to do – to share Christ with those who lived within it. And so, the work began to grow.

CT made Nala his headquarters and sent staff off to Niangara, Poko and Bambili to set up bases there. The area contained ten tribes and was about half the size of England. In April 1917, CT was to write home:

> The work here is a marvel, quite beyond my conception.
> The finger of God is writ all over it. We arrived here two
> strangers three and a half years ago, the natives sunk in
> sin unprintable, the medium of communication to be
> learned, yet there are now just upon 100 baptised converts
> … everywhere we have an open door for ourselves and our
> native Christians. [6]

In 1917 the Belgian Government ratified the concession to the Mission and made CT an intermediary between it and the Government. A boys' school was started, and shortly afterwards another for girls.

The new converts loved to pray and so a daily 5.30 am prayer meeting was started. So eager were the people to attend that often the singing would start half an hour early. Then came the prayers … and what prayers they prayed! They often prayed for CT, though not quite as he expected them to:

And there's Bwana, Lord … he is a very aged man (he was 60 at the time), his strength is no use, give him yours as well Lord, and the Holy Ghost as well. Oh Lord, you have been indeed good to have caused Bwana to live ten years on earth, now cause him to live two more years.

Baptismal services were very special as candidates publicly declared their faith in front of the entire village they lived in. CT made sure each person was carefully spoken with, to ensure they knew what they were doing and really had a testimony to share.

The Africans loved to sing. The hymns had mainly been composed by Alfred to fit their understanding. One such hymn translated into English said:

> *The road to hell is broad,*
> *The devil keeps it well swept.*
> *Very many people travel on it,*
> *Because madness has seized them.*
>
> *The road to heaven is difficult,*
> *There is a stream to cross.*
> *But there is only one canoe to ferry you over,*
> *The name of the canoe is Jesus.[7]*

Another hymn they loved to sing with great gusto to a popular Salvation Army tune was:

> *There are no taxes to pay in heaven.*
> *One can rest there gratuitously.*
> *Of soldiers and judges and prisons and courts of law,*
> *And cat-o-nine tails there is not one,*

THE CONGO ONCE MORE

Let us go, let us go, to the village of God
The village of joy and love.

Soon some of those who had been baptised came to CT and said
they wanted to go out and tell others about Jesus. The principle of
making disciples and then them going out to share the good news
with others was happening. The sending out of volunteer natives
was a lesson to CT in how to evangelise an area. He wrote:

> We white evangelists have five porters each to carry our
> necessities; they carry their own. Each (white) man or
> woman carries a bed, but theirs consists solely of a grass
> mat; their bedding consists of a thin blanket, if they have
> one at all; the only lunch basket they possess is always out
> of sight and beneath a belt, from which hangs a jungle
> knife and an enamel cup. A straw hat on their head of their
> own make, a loin cloth, and you have the Heart of Africa
> missionary complete.[8]

Initially twenty of the new African Christians volunteered to go
and evangelise their regions. As they prepared to go, CT wanted to
remind them how to be victorious in the work:

> If you don't desire to meet the devil during the day, meet
> Jesus before dawn. If you don't want the devil to hit you,
> hit him first and hit him with all your might, so that he
> may be too crippled to hit back. 'Preach the Word' is the
> rod the devil fears and hates.[9]

The new missionaries were sent out for a month, two months,
three months, depending how long they could last. They were each
given three francs to cover their board, keep and travel expenses
whilst they were away. Amazingly some had money left over when

they returned at the end of the three-month Mission trip. Their exploits encouraged others to want to go. From the first three-month Mission trip, fifty men asked for baptism.

On 10 October 1918, CT wrote:

> The progress is simply wonderful. People are coming to us from every quarter and from very long distances. We are having pretty nearly weekly baptisms. The converts are evangelising far and near. Now Chiefs are imploring us to send them teachers and are even building chapels and houses for us.

In the same letter he wrote: 'Four men came a twenty-day journey to Nala and when asked why, said, "All the world knows there is much knowledge of God at Nala".'[10]

When CT had travelled from the Congo River to Nala, he had come via an unusual route through the province of Ituri. As he journeyed, a chief had met him and offered him a beautiful plot of land if he would come and teach them. It was situated on a hill called Deti and in time became the first Mission station in the Ituri province.

One of the feared chiefs of the area was a cannibal who had reportedly eaten fourteen natives. When his wife heard the missionaries speak, she said: 'I always said there ought to be a God like that.'

Out of the group who had come from England were a Mr and Mrs Ellis. They agreed to go and pioneer a new work in the area. CT visited them in June 1918 for a weekend and wrote about his visit.

> When it was time for Church I went to the – well, I suppose I must call it a Church, though it was just a grass

hut ... I found the place simply packed with black shiny bodies ... the service began. It was in Kingwana and so was an unknown tongue as far as I was concerned.

The singing was remarkably good and accurate ... Then the Lord's Prayer, and another passage of Scripture, all interspersed with hymns.

Then came my turn. I had to give them a talk ... I began a bit nervously. I hate interpreter speaking ... I decided to speak as though I ne'er shall preach again. And as a dying man to dying men. It seemed absolutely impossible to speak sentence by sentence, so I fired off now short and now long and had to trust to the interpreter to catch the sense and re-telling it aright. ...

Then a hymn and Ellis spoke a few words, and the great service was over... My mind wandered back to just one year ago, when Deti was only a hill top bare of everything but the elephant grass and the jungle undergrowth of Africa. Alfred, and the Ellis's and I had gone to inspect (Chief) Abiengama's gift of the hill top, to thank God for His gift of the place in which to begin our work. ... My heart drummed with the message, 'This is the finger of God and what hath God wrought ...'[11]

CT hurried back from Deti to Nala where he knew his daughter Edith was about to give birth. Fortunately he arrived before baby Susan made her entrance into the world. A great prayer time was held to give thanks for her birth.

After three years out in the Congo, it became time for more separation and for some of the team to return to the UK. It was six years since Alfred, as a young man of only twenty-one years of age, had travelled to Africa with CT. He had stayed there for the two years, whilst CT had returned to the UK. Now it was his time to return to the UK for a while, with his wife and daughter. CT was to say of him: 'None but God can ever know the deep fellowship, joy and affection of our daily, social and spiritual communion, for no words can describe it.'[12]

On the day Alfred left Nala with his wife and baby daughter, the whole of the village came to wave goodbye. In the end it took them three hours to leave because so many people were wanting to say goodbyes and give handshakes. As he was about to depart Alfred asked CT to lay his hands on him and pray for him. CT said he would if Alfred would do as he asked. Surprised, Alfred agreed so CT replied, 'Please stand on your chair.'

Not sure what was happening, Alfred did so. CT stooped down and laid his hands on his feet. The tears flowed as he asked God to protect Alfred, Edith and Susan and bring them back home to Nala. With their farewells said, they departed leaving CT in charge.

Returning to the UK with Alfred and his wife, were four of the missionaries who needed a furlough, and wanted time back in England. Their departures meant there was only a little band of six left behind in the Congo. They found themselves severely tested. CT especially felt a sense of loneliness with Alfred and Edith gone.

Stoically the group faced the challenges posed by the decrease in staffing. Ill health was a major problem but so too was that caused by the backsliding of a number of local Africans who had made commitments. Many of these had been identified as possible leaders in the future. In May 1920 CT wrote to his mother about the problem of backsliding: 'I think disappointments are the greatest sufferings.'[13]

Health-wise he was struggling considerably, too. In the same letter he wrote: 'I have been having an awful time with terrible irritation of the arms and legs, and many bad ulcers on the feet and ankles; the irritation is sometimes maddening.'[14]

The group spread themselves out as best they could, with one at Deti, one at Poko, one in Ituri and Bwana, and two ladies, Nurse Amall, (who in time became Mrs Staniford), and Miss Bromberger at Nala.

On the Home Front

Back in the UK, the First World War had finished. CT and Priscilla's daughter Dorothy, along with her husband Gilbert, had joined the team at the Mission headquarters at 17 Highland Road in Upper Norwood, South London. Gilbert had been given the title of Home Overseer and helper to Priscilla, a role he was to fulfil for the next eight years. He ran with CT's vision for an 'all of the world' mission, not just one limited to the Congo. It was Gilbert's initiative for the Mission to change its name to the 'Worldwide Evangelization Crusade', which in time was shortened to 'WEC International'. The use of the word 'Crusade' was intentional. For CT it implied fighting and self-dedicating sacrifice, which were so important to him. However, the name was changed again to 'Worldwide Evangelisation for Christ'. There was concern the word 'Crusade' might be misunderstood, because of past historical actions, which had not reflected Christian love for all people.

Whilst CT was the leader of the Mission and its face in Africa, Priscilla was very much its leader in the UK. To her fell the tasks of promoting the Mission, keeping it functioning correctly, raising the funds that kept her husband and the other missionaries on the mission field. She was also responsible for raising awareness of the need for more missionaries to go to the unreached regions of the world.[15]

Priscilla did not find her life easy. Those who were close to her knew how difficult she found the separation and sacrifice they had made as a family. She struggled with feelings of rejection, loneliness, and the loss of her personal calling, though she never allowed her personal feelings to get in the way of the work.

When CT had been in the UK, he had written to Alfred about the change in Priscilla: 'I cannot say what joy it gives me. She is now like what she used to be in China. I have never seen anyone to compare with her – man or woman – when she gets going: she has such energy and vision and faith that she can capture anyone.'[16]

In the early days of the Mission, 17 Highland Road was more than able to handle all its work. But, as the home staff grew, guests visited, new recruits arrived and returning missionaries dropped by, plus all the literature and books for distribution that were stored in the place, there was hardly any room to move. CT in his book, *Reminiscences of Mrs C T Studd*, wrote:

Mrs Studd's hospitality at 17 Highland Road, made it an ever-open house to the servants of God, and none were more welcome there than the foreign missionary while seeking rest and change at home, and the young man or woman bent on leaving the homeland for the 'regions beyond.'[17]

One day, Priscilla challenged the cook to pray for a garage next door to their house to become empty and available for them to use. It did become empty but was then used as a Cats and Dogs Home. Finally the people left and it became available to rent again. Priscilla was hesitant at committing the Mission to more expense but knew she did not dare say no. The Mission subsequently rented number 19, so that 17 and 19 Highland Road became available for Mission use. Sometime later they were able to purchase the property. A friend of the Mission, Miss L Gristwood, bought a house on the opposite side of Highland Road. She bought it for herself to live in, but also for use as an additional WEC Mission house.

In 1919, Priscilla and the Home Committee in faith wrote to CT and declared 'Reinforcements leaving this year'. As they sent the declaration they had no new recruits to send to the mission field. But seven days before the end of December 1919, the first group of new recruits left England for the Congo. Amongst them was CT and Priscilla's youngest daughter, Pauline, and her husband, Norman Grubb.

In early 1920, two more groups of recruits departed the UK shores for Africa. Within three years, the six missionaries who were serving overseas had grown to almost forty.

CHAPTER 12

Running a Mission

Africa 1921 Onwards

In 1921, Alfred and Edith Buxton knew it was time for them to return to the Belgian Congo, and especially to Nala where they had been based. They made great sacrifice in deciding to leave their two children in the care of Alfred's mother. Both children struggled with chest complaints and doctors had warned the parents that two-and-a-half-year-old Susan and baby Lionel would be in grave danger if they were taken to the Congo. As Alfred and Edith settled back in Nala, CT sensed a release to move on and pioneer more areas. He certainly had no thoughts of taking a break in the UK, even though he walked with a stoop and had teeth problems.

Four days march south of Nala, through virgin forest in the Ituri region, was a village named Ibambi in the Ituri Forest. The place was teeming with people. The people appeared so happy but, scratch the surface, and underneath was cruelty, uncleanness, greediness, witchcraft, fear, murder and beastliness. Marriage was purely a business transaction. They had no concept of holiness or heaven and had never heard of a God who loves and cares, and who could wash their hearts clean. In 1920 one of the missionaries, James Lowder, went into the area to work alongside CT. Along with Congolese workers who accompanied him, he did a remarkable work of evangelising among the Budu people around Wamba and Ibambi. The area became one of the richest harvest fields. Because of the reports of the amazing response to the gospel that were happening in the area, CT went to see the area and work for himself. He decided to make the area his home.

CT therefore moved his headquarters to Ibambi in 1922 and settled there. He was to stay here until his dying day. The local people's name for him of *Bwana Mukubwa* (Great White Chief) became his name, which in time was shortened to *Bwana*. They loved having him in their midst, with his gaunt appearance, thick beard, smile and laugh.

Amongst the people CT found there was a rich hunger for the things of God. To them it was nothing to walk one, two, or even eight hours, through the forest to hear God's Word explained to them. They began to come in their hundreds to Ibambi to be taught and baptised. In all his years in mission, CT had never known such a hunger for the gospel. He was not to know that, in time, hundreds would come to faith in Christ under his ministry there; a church would be built to hold 1,250 and it would not be large enough to fit everyone in.

CT's home was built next to the first church on the site. It was a circular hut, made of split bamboos, tied together with string with a grass roof and dried mud floor. In one of the corners was a bed covered with goats' hide over a wooden frame. It had been given to him by the local Chief. Near his bed was a homemade table for all his gadgets – scissors, knives, medicines, papers, clock, and spectacles. A special space was reserved for his Bibles. He used the Revised Version and aimed to have a new one every year. Old notes and comments were of no use to him. He wanted fresh manna every year ... every day ... from the Lord.

At the foot of his bed was an open log fire to warm him on the cold nights. Sharing his room with him, and lying as close to the fire as possible was his 'boy' In fact he was a grown man who cared for CT's needs on a daily basis. Between 2.30 am and 3.00 am his 'boy' would awake. He would go to the fire, knock off the burned ends of the log, blow gently into the fire until the sparks turn to flames, then put the kettle on the fire and make a cup of tea, which he would hand to Bwana, who by this time, was awake.

The 'boy' would then go back to sleep. Bwana would take his Bible and spend time alone with God for several hours. What God said to him during those early mornings would form the basis of what he shared in talks at devotional times and in prayer meetings during the day. The Word was alive to him. CT often said to young missionaries: 'Don't go into your study to prepare a sermon. That is all nonsense. Go into your study to go to God and get so fiery that your tongue is like a burning coal and you've got to speak.'[1]

His days were consumed with so much activity. At times he drove those around him crazy with his micro-managing of tasks. Things had to be right for *Bwana*. He believed it so important that good Christians were not lazy and that Christians showed themselves to be good workmen in all they did.

As head of the Mission there were always tasks that demanded his time – correspondence to answer, accounts to be checked, people to see. Every other Saturday was European mail day. He would save up letters from home until that Saturday and then spend the whole day sitting at his desk answering them. Often it was late in the evening before he finished. Then the post would be packed up, a runner found, given a lantern and a spear, and off the person would go on a twelve-hour journey through the forest to pass the post on to the post-person leaving from Wamba.

As he finished the post, a team of men would be waiting outside CT's hut ready to take him on his visits. He would put a few necessities together – lamp, Bible, papers, a few medicines, blanket, some tins of European food that had been sent for him. The tins were not for his personal use but for him to pass on to the missionaries he would be visiting.

He hated to be carried when he travelled but, as the years progressed and his body physically could not cope so well, he reluctantly had to agree to a *mandala* (carrying chair)

There would be a man at the front with a spear and lantern, four carriers, two at the front and two at the rear, and another team of four to relieve the carriers. They would sing as they travelled. After four or five hours travelling they would stop and shelter somewhere and catch a little sleep. They did not want to arrive at the Mission station before 6.00 am.

The people would hear news of CT's coming to their area by the beating of the hollow wooden drums. The distant boom of the prayer drum would travel through the forest, and villages would hurriedly get up and prepare for their journey to where he was.

A service lasting one or two hours would be held in the morning for the missionaries and the local Christians. Then CT would relax and eat breakfast whilst the missionaries would share news and talk over problems with him.

The main service of the day would be at midday. Despite the intensity of the heat, it had to be in the open air and often as many as 2,000 would be present. There were no buildings that could hold the crowds. Palm fronds held up on poles would try to protect the people from the sun.

The people loved the hymn singing. They were mainly hymns written by *Bwana* and Alfred, and he would lead 'singing with his banjo'. The prayer time in the services could last for forty minutes as one after another led the prayers. Each prayer finished with the entire congregation saying '*Ku jinoya Yesu*' (in the name of Jesus).

When it was time for *Bwana* to speak, he would stand on a raised piece of earth and read the Scriptures to them. He would make the passage relevant to their situation – bread became bananas, camels became elephants, the people had black skins and bark cloth. The people listened in rapt attention as he spoke for an hour, or even two, on occasions. Then another hymn, an invitation to the people to respond to Jesus. The end of the meeting would be when all the people stood, raised their hands in the air and declared 'God is, Jesus is, coming quickly. Hallelujah.'

Some of the people would have to leave but the majority had brought their sleeping mats and settled down for the night wherever they could find a sleeping space. Monday would then be a repeat of Sunday with one or two services. The meetings might even continue into the Tuesday.

New Teeth

As CT's body became weaker, he had much trouble with his teeth. The few that remained became rotten and he could not consume anything that was not in a liquid form. Whenever the subject came up, some of the missionaries would say to him: 'CT, you really ought to go back to the UK and sort your teeth out.'

The reply was always the same: 'If God wants me to have some new teeth, he can just as easily send me some here.'

Everyone would laugh a little. But God heard that prayer.

Around this time, a dentist in England applied to join the Heart of Africa Mission. Unfortunately, his age was against him, and the Home Committee declined his application. However, the dentist concerned was not put off. Ignoring the Committee's advice, he sold his practice in London and used the money to buy a ticket for passage to the Congo. He arrived at the coast, but unfortunately did not have enough money to travel into the interior.

The dentist therefore decided to earn more money by setting up a dental practice in the area, attending to the teeth of the officials and traders. After a few months he had sufficient funds to carry on his journey into the interior.

It so happened that CT's youngest daughter, Pauline, and her husband, Norman Grubb, were travelling back to England. As Pauline and her husband were canoeing down the Aruwimi River, toward where it joins the Congo, they saw a canoe coming in the opposite direction. They were even more surprised to see a white man in it. That was an unusual occurrence in the Congo! Not knowing anything about the person, they called out a greeting in English and were amazed to receive a reply in the same language.

The two canoes stopped on the side of the river and the occupants suggested some breakfast together. To the astonishment of Pauline and her husband, the gentleman told them that his name was Mr Buck and God had told him to go and join Mr Studd. He confided in Pauline that God had told him not only was he to go to Africa to preach the gospel, but also to sort out CT's teeth. With that in mind he had in his luggage a new set of teeth and all the equipment necessary for making and fitting them!

Mr Buck left Pauline and her husband as they went their opposite ways and, in due time, in the rainy season of 1921, Mr Buck found C T Studd. It had taken him a year and a half since selling his practice to get there. When CT told the story, he said:

> When Buck arrived, the first thing he said to me was 'God has sent me to the Congo to sort your teeth out.' Just fancy God sending a dentist to the very heart of Africa to look after the teeth of His child, who could not return home. What, I wondered, would God not do?[2]

Over the coming weeks, John Buck extracted CT's rotten stubs and moulded a set of false teeth for him.

One Sunday morning, soon after the dentist had worked on CT's teeth, *Bwana* attended a service with 1,000 locals. As he stood up to speak with his shiny white teeth on display, there was bewilderment, awe, wonder and astonishment by those who were there at what they were seeing. *'Bwana's* got new teeth. Hallelujah. Isn't God good!'

But there was a problem. The plate did not fit properly and, as the service progressed, it became very sore in his mouth. During the prayer time CT removed the plate, causing huge astonishment from those in the congregation when he stood up to sing the next song. His teeth had disappeared during the prayer time. How could that have happened?

From that point on, every time he appeared, people wanted to check. Had he got white shiny teeth or was it the old *Bwana* with no teeth? The teeth became a feature in themselves and CT milked it. On one occasion, when surrounded by some children, he sat on a low stool with his teeth in. He took a pair of pliers and in front of all the children pulled out eight teeth all in one go![3]

However hard John Buck tried, that first set of teeth never quite fitted properly and CT took to leaving them around on his table beside his bed. That was fine but he almost got caught out one day when an important official arrived to see him. Fortunately CT just made it back to his room to put his teeth in before the official appeared.

Growth

The number of new recruits from the UK continued to increase. There were forty missionaries serving with the Mission by 1923, making a total number of fifty staff when foreign workers were included. From Ibambi CT and his team began to move out. In Adzangwe, which was three hours' trek away, five or six hundred eagerly gathered to hear about the living God. The same was true at other centres, such as Badua, Bakondangama, and Adzoka. New stations also opened at Wamba, Botonwe, Bomili and Panga.

Inevitably there was opposition to the outreaches, but the opposition only served to increase interest in the work. This particularly was seen when hostility was shown to those who volunteered to be local evangelists. One evangelist was beaten for witnessing in a village. When the beating was over, he stood up, extended his hand to the chief, and thanked him for allowing him to be beaten for Jesus. In another village an evangelist was put in the local jail. His new converts gathered at the jail clamouring for the honour of being locked up as well.

The new recruits to the Heart of Africa Mission were drawn

from all walks of life. On one occasion CT said: 'Why seek higher education? … What we need is a bricklayer who will talk about Christ. He doesn't need theology.'[4] However he also understood the need to train new recruits. In 1921 the Mission commenced the Missionary Training Colony in Upper Norwood, London, with the focus on Bible Study, practical work, missionary principles, prayer and evangelism. Alfred's brother, Captain Godfrey Buxton, had been severely injured during the First World War and was unable himself to go on the mission field. He agreed to lead the new training work[5].

To all new recruits to the mission, one of the warnings that CT gave to them was:

> The hearts of men are desperately wicked and we know
> very little about them. Don't be taken in by the devil, nor
> by yourself, nor by men. A man or woman, white or black,
> must be full of the Holy Ghost if he or she is to stand, and
> not be lost in sin out here.[6]

The sacraments of Baptism and the Lord's Supper were an important part of the church services on a Sunday morning. The Lord's Supper consisted of slices of banana (bread was unknown among the Africans) and water coloured pink with permanganate of potash to resemble wine (a typical C T Studd substitute). CT became aware, after a number of years of fast growth, that nationals were coming for baptism and communion with lives still involved in pagan practices. He therefore suspended all sacraments in Mission churches until the new converts learnt that practical holiness was more important than ceremony.[7]

Many years later Norman Grubb was to describe CT as a 'holiness preacher'[8]. To CT, holiness was a simple matter. If you have the Holy Spirit in you, you live a holy life. He vehemently opposed any teaching which allowed a person to be saved and en-route to heaven, who also lived in sin. However, he did not presume that a person could reach perfection. He understood the will still had to be applied, as an assertion of a person's faith, in allowing Christ's resurrection life to dominate their actions.

Within ten years of the mission's formation, medical, industrial and education work was underway, translations of the Bible had been made, books and hymn books published, elders and evangelists appointed and an estimated 9,000 converts, of whom 4,000 had been baptised. When Priscilla spoke at an event at London's Central Hall in 1922, she said the provision of workers and money had been amazing, and the Mission had representation, not only in the UK, but also in North America, Australia, New Zealand and South Africa.[9]

Tension Within – The Americans

The idea behind changing the name from Heart of Africa Mission to Worldwide Evangelization Crusade, was to fulfil the vision of reaching the whole world with the message of Jesus Christ.

The Home Committee recognised the importance of America if they were to see the vision fulfilled. They had many contacts there. CT's older brother, Kynaston, had worked there in establishing the Student Christian Movement and CT was well known and liked through the tours of the US that he had done.

In 1920 the Committee therefore decided the way to move America forward was for some of the team to go there and promote the work. There was no way that CT would move from Africa so he was out of the question. Since Priscilla had spent considerable time and effort building up the American base for the mission, she was an obvious choice to go. Alfred had spent six years pioneering the work in Africa with CT and was available, so it was agreed that he should go with her. Alfred's wife, Edith (CT and Priscilla's daughter), was about to give birth to their second child and so could not travel. She stayed in the UK and in time had a lovely baby boy whom they called Lionel. The purpose of the tour of the USA was to recruit missionaries and raise financial support.

It was a successful tour and a WEC USA office was established. There was great rejoicing when it was announced that seven recruits were going to join the work in Africa from the USA.

By the time these new recruits arrived in Africa in 1924, Alfred and Edith were back in the Congo. Alfred had met some of the new recruits during the USA tour and personally recommended them as suitable for missionary work. He was therefore very pleased to see them again. However, sadly CT was not impressed.

Until the arrival of the Americans, all of the WEC missionaries in the Congo had come from the United Kingdom and primarily from mainline denominations such as the Presbyterians and Methodists. The Americans were mainly Baptists. Soon after their arrival, arguments began to develop between the British and American missionaries over the interpretation of certain passages in the Bible and points of doctrine. The Americans claimed to be 'Calvinists' believing 'once saved, always saved.' CT took an opposing view, believing 'holiness of life and a hatred of sin were the fruit of repentance, to be continually evidenced before new birth could be assumed.'[10] As far as CT was concerned, a man could lose his salvation at any time.

As the leader of the mission, it might have been wise for CT to seek reconciliation between the disagreeing parties. He didn't. He forcibly came down on the side of the British missionaries. He had his views and was not going to change from them.

Within a few weeks the American WEC missionaries declared that they could not be a part of the Mission and left, never to return. In the territory adjacent to the WEC work, there was the American missionary society called the Africa Inland Mission. They applied there and were all accepted.

The period after their departure was not a pleasant time for the mission. Initially everyone was stunned, but then the accusations began to fly. Alfred felt particularly hurt. He had been the one who had gone to the USA and encouraged the Americans to join the mission. He felt they had been badly treated. He particularly felt that CT could have done more to bring harmony to the situation, rather than add to the discord. The UK Home Committee could not understand CT's attitude, and blamed him for the Americans' departure. Priscilla, as secretary of the Home Committee, had the difficult task of trying to convey to CT how they felt, and who they blamed for the Americans not staying!

The situation was further exasperated when the departing American missionaries sent a report back to their home base – the USA office of WEC – of the way they had been treated. Soon letters were flying from the USA office threatening to withdraw their support and suggesting they might become an independent organisation.

As the tension grew between the WEC offices in the UK and USA, as well as the workers in the field in the Congo, the UK Home Committee arranged in 1927 for Alfred Buxton, with his wife Edith, to go to the USA to try to repair the relationship with American supporters.

The first that CT knew of it was a letter from Alfred telling him he and Edith were in America, trying to explain and soothe things over. CT was not consulted about their trip and was furious. He believed the fault lay entirely with the Americans and it was their disagreeable attitude which had caused all the problems.

He resented Alfred and Edith being in America to do 'smooth talking' with the supporters over there so he fired off a letter to Alfred and Edith. He told Alfred that he was showing disloyalty to him as the founder and that he should consider himself dismissed from the mission. As for Edith, his daughter, he told her she need never return to the Congo. Alfred –the same Alfred who had ventured out with CT when he had first journeyed to the Congo to established the Heart of Africa mission, and who had so loyally served the cause for thirteen years – was shocked.[11] The missionaries working in the Congo were similarly affected when they heard the news of what CT had done. Tensions were beginning to grow within the movement and they were not good for the work.

Further Tensions and Conflict

Opposition began to grow to CT. It was not only from the local witch doctors, who did not like him or his message. Beneath the surface the tensions within the Mission were mounting. Pressure was increasing on CT to spend some time in the UK for many different reasons. Priscilla hadn't seen him for many years and wanted him to return home. Furthermore, he would not let her visit him in the Congo. Also, CT's health demanded he return so that he could obtain medical advice. Finally, the Home Committee urgently wanted to meet with him to discuss the onward direction of the mission.

Many around CT felt it was right for him to leave the Congo and return to the UK. But not CT. It became a major problem. Whenever pressures built on him to return to the UK – either permanently because of his health, or temporarily to have some rest, CT always had the same reply: 'What go home? Never! God told me to come and he hasn't told me to go.'[12] How do you argue with that?

To one person he wrote:

How can I spend the best years of my life living for
the honours of this world, when thousands of souls are
perishing every day? Forty years ago, at God's command,
I left mother, brethren, friends, fortune and all that is
usually thought to make life worth living ... I don't think
I should much enjoy ending up being frightened out of
doing my duty by hearkening to the comments of men.
'Cursed is he that trusteth in man' does not make a very
good pillow for a dying man, but there is much comfort in
the other one. 'Blessed is he that trusteth in the Lord'.[13]

It had been good to have family involved in the Mission – until the falling out happened.

Alfred Buxton had pioneered the work with him in the Congo. Now CT felt Alfred was trying to undermine his authority. Accusingly he wrote to the Home Committee: 'It looks as if Alfred is the loving one – I am the ogre.'[14]

Another daughter, Pauline, and her husband Norman Grubb, were similarly struggling in their relationship with CT – and they were in the Congo with him. Once when CT contracted a serious illness, Pauline assumed she, as his daughter, would be the one to nurse him. However, CT preferred another missionary to do it and told Norman and Pauline to go and do some Mission work at a far-away station.

Differences also arose between the team of missionaries who were working alongside CT. It was not CT's best gifting to lead and administrate. His heart was evangelism. Some of those who served with him described him as obstinate, an unreasonable leader and colleague, who provoked bitter conflict within his family, fellow missionaries and even the Africans that he went to serve. Some opposed his strong emphasis on practical holiness and thought he was being too hard on those who made commitments to Christ.

Every missionary who came to the Congo had made great sacrifice to be there, yet CT wanted to run the Mission like a military machine. He would scold any who wanted time off for relaxation. As far as CT was concerned the Mission was founded on 'simple faith and supreme sacrifice.' He expected fellow missionaries to live in native-built houses, to eat plain food, to have no days off, no relaxation time and totally live for the task of reaching those in their community. He could not understand other nearby missions, such as the Baptist Missionary Society, who encouraged their workers to 'actually take annual holidays, and play tennis on Saturday afternoons, instead of spending every moment fighting the devil.'[15]

Anyone who tried to argue with CT found it was impossible to disagree with him and remain friends with him. To those who criticised him, CT's response was:

I am getting very fearful lest fizz and froth take the place of the Divine fire amongst us ... I find there is far more talk and time given to food than there should be: and I find

197

too often that the original foundation of supreme sacrifice gives place to self-pleasing ... our intensity must ever increase.[16]

The disagreements reached a point where CT dismissed two of the missionaries. A number of others resigned and increasingly Alfred found himself siding with those CT was falling out with.

Whilst all this was going on Pauline and Norman's son, Noel Grubb, was born. The grandchild was to live just one year. On his first birthday, he was buried at Nala, in the Democratic Republic of the Congo.

A Broken Marriage?

From this distance of time it is hard to know what happened to CT and Priscilla's marriage. Can a marriage exist where neither partner has seen the other for at least thirteen years? Certainly, when it started it had been so tender and passionate. That can be seen in the language of the letters between the two of them when they were apart in their early years. But how could it survive years of them living in separate countries? Priscilla felt a loneliness and rejection; CT had left the UK against her wishes. She was caught in the middle of all the nastiness with the Home Committee. As far as CT was concerned, he always loved her and saw the separation as one more sacrifice he had to make for the sake of God's mission.

Priscilla, whatever her personal feelings, was always an advocate for him, and gave herself totally to support and raise funds and personnel for the mission. When they had married, she had worn a sash proclaiming 'United to fight for Jesus.' Despite Priscilla's best efforts, they were not united and they spent very little time together in the work of the gospel. As death approached CT did not want to share the experience with his wife or have her near him. They both were to die alone from each other.

Don't Care a Damn

The fledging Mission faced its biggest crisis when CT decided to launch his DCD campaign. He had heard a retired military man use the phrase to describe his passion and dedication for King and Country. In his autocratic way he expected all the staff and volunteers of the Mission to sign up to it. DCD stood for 'Don't Care a Damn,' though the Home Committee tried to suggest it stood for 'I don't care if I die for Christ. '

According to CT, 'A DCD (was) a soldier of Jesus Christ who (didn't) care a damn for anything but Him and the salvation of souls.'[17]

The Mission ladies were asked to create a flag with a cross emblazoned on it, red against white. The letters S V were to be embroidered on it, which stood for 'Safi Vita' (Holy War). That's how CT saw what was happening. He was declaring a holy war.

The DCD booklet declared: 'God is looking for men who couldn't care less about anything but Christ Himself and His gospel.'

As a furore over the language CT was using increased, he was unmoved. He believed he was saying the same as Paul when he wrote in Philippians 3:8: 'I have suffered the loss of all things, and count them as rubbish, that I may gain Christ.'

The booklet that CT wrote to go with the campaign, was called The DCD. On its front cover was a gruesome skull and cross bones. The language used in the booklet might be considered mildly expletive today. However, it was certainly not the language the Christian public in the early 1900s were used to hearing and reading. The Home Committee refused to publish it. CT published it anyway, privately, and sent it out. He went as far as saying that the DCD 'was God-given, and it was God's great new thing for the age.'[18] Many supporters were scandalised by it. They could not understand what was going on and stopped giving to the work. Funds for the Mission dramatically dried up.

To make sense of it all we need to step back a little. CT never claimed to be your typical Christian missionary. He believed in plain speaking. His gifting first of all was as an evangelist who could be very blunt in the way he expressed things. In his famous thirty-two-page booklet called *The Chocolate Soldier,* he wrote:

> God's real people have always been called fanatics. Jesus was called mad; so was Paul, so was Whitfield, Wesley, Moody, Spurgeon. No one has graduated far in God's school who has not been paid the compliment of being called a fanatic.[19]

In the book he compares real soldiers of Christ to the chocolate soldiers of his day.

> To the chocolate soldier the very thought of war brings a violent attack of ague, while the call to battle always finds him with the palsy.[20]

When CT launched the 'Don't Care a Damn' campaign, what he was really challenging Christians to do, was make a statement declaring: 'Henceforth I don't give a damn for anything, save the glory of Jesus, obedience to God, and the evangelisation of the world.' Where things came unstuck was the way in which he did it. He took delight in shocking strait-laced people and many thought his eccentricity had gone too far.

There was one more area that was to cause difficulties for the Mission during the latter years of CT's life. This was an accusation that he had become addicted to drugs, particularly morphine.

Why were so many of CT's friends – including his wife, his family, and the Home Committee – encouraging him to return to the UK? It was because they could see that he was struggling with many ailments and needed professional help. These included gallstones, swelling to his hands and feet, a heart problem, enlarged liver and congested lungs. His close friend and former physician, Dr A T Wilkinson, had been aware of his condition for twenty-five years, and said: 'He was a museum of diseases when he left China and was afterwards hardly ever free.'[21]

Those who advised him to return to the UK honestly believed he needed to receive proper medical treatment, so that he would be relieved of much of the severe pains that were afflicting him. However, CT would have none of it. All his life he had looked after himself and been his own doctor. In his medical bag, as in most missionary bags at the time, were morphine and quinine. When his pain became too much, CT's solution was to take a shot of morphine. It relieved malaria, headaches, heart pain and the agony of gallstones.

He made no attempt to hide taking the morphine and would openly take a shot in front of other missionaries. Because he lived in Africa, he had to ask the Home Committee to send the drugs to him and they were reluctant to do so. Somehow news of CT's drug-taking leaked out to the public and this became another reason for people to stop supporting the mission. CT could not understand the fuss. He wrote:

God works in wonderful ways. I was bad with fever and in bed with a temperature of 102.6. Crowds came so I gave myself a shot of morphine. I went out, took the meeting which lasted five hours or more, came back smiling, with no temperature at all … People are getting right with God at considerable sacrifice.[22]

In 1928, it was thought that CT was going to die. As he lay in his bed struggling for breath, those who saw him were sure the end was close. Some of the team were able to contact the Belgian Red Cross. A doctor came who treated him with various drugs including morphine. Gradually strength returned to him but not enough to enable him to get out of his bed and certainly not to begin work again, without daily dosing himself on the drugs.

To CT he had a choice. He could be an invalid, bed-ridden and needing one or more missionaries to look after him, or he could take the drugs and have the strength to work and preach. He therefore found doctors who were sympathetic to his peculiar circumstances and would prescribe him the drugs. As a storm raged over his drug-taking, CT declared: 'I have never taken it for pleasure. It is part of the sacrifice of serving the Master.'[23]

Another area for criticism was over his relationship with his son-in-law. Alfred Buxton, who as a 20-year-old had first travelled with CT, tried reconciliation with him but it was not to be. Alfred even travelled to Ibambi to meet with CT and talk with him but CT refused his olive branch. As far as he was concerned, Alfred should have been coming to ask for his forgiveness but Alfred did not even understand, or remember, what he was supposed to have done wrong.

There were times when CT felt vulnerable, lonely, and really could not understand why his actions attracted criticism. In one of his letters to Priscilla, he wrote:

> Sometimes I feel, and especially of late, that my cross is heavy beyond endurance, and I fear I often feel like fainting under it, but I hope to go on and not faint. My heart seems worn out and bruised beyond repair, and in my deep loneliness I often wish to be gone, but God knows best, and I want to do every ounce of work He wants me to do.[24]

Decisive Action by the Home Committee

The Home Committee members were struggling to know how to proceed. Supporters were asking questions they did not know the answers to and funds were diminishing and so there was less money for sending to the Field, to support the missionaries. A pattern was emerging where missionaries were doing one term of service in the Congo, coming home on furlough and then not returning or worse (certainly in CT's eyes) were transferring to another mission. The final straw, as far as the Home Committee was concerned, was a letter they received from CT telling them that every member of the Home Committee had to be a declared 'DCD' or be out.

CT wanted the DCD booklet to be prominently displayed at all deputation meetings, for all staff to wear a uniform with the skull and cross bones as a badge, and the words 'I don't care a damn for anything but Jesus Christ' be embroidered on the hat. He informed the Home Committee that, if they sent any worker to the field who was not signed up as a declared DCD, he would send them home again.

The Home Committee knew they had to do something. They started by asking those missionaries who were home on furlough to meet with them and talk about their experiences in the Congo. One of the first to do so was Victor Evening who was touring the UK, speaking at deputation meetings as part of his furlough, after seven years in the Congo working alongside CT.

After meeting the Committee, he was asked to meet with other furlough missionaries and gather their opinion. He arranged a meeting with a Mr and Mrs Kerrigan, Mr and Mrs Fripp, Mr Gilbert Buckley (his wife had just had a baby and could not attend) and a Miss Allen. The Home Committee concluded that CT was ruining the Mission that he had started. Even though they understood that CT would not back down, they drafted a letter to send to him. Amongst their points were:

- DCD had begun as an option now he was making it compulsory
- He was turning a slogan into an article of faith
- Non-DCD's were being treated as inferior Christians

The Committee pleaded for moderation but in their hearts knew all the letter would do was rouse the wrath of CT.

Another emergency meeting was called and Gilbert Buckley and Victor Evening were asked to attend, to share the views of those on furlough. This they did and a draft of the proposed letter to be sent to CT was read out. Gilbert and Victor were asked to withdraw whilst the Committee deliberated.

When the men returned to the meeting they were told that the Committee wanted to send a deputation of four to meet with CT in the Congo, to try to reason with him. The Committee wanted the four to consist of two Committee members and two missionaries on furlough. The Rev Arthur Thynne, a Committee member and a Baptist Minister would lead the four along with a fellow Committee member and businessman, Mr Emory. They then asked Gilbert Buckley and Victor Evening, both of whom had served with CT for more than seven years in the Congo, to be the other two members of the group.

The Committee made a pledge that, if the deputation was not successful in reasoning with CT, they would resign en-masse and support any of the missionaries at home on furlough, or in the field, in the starting of a new mission.

With today's means of travel, the visit should have been held within a matter of a few weeks. In the 1920s it took many months to organise and then travel to the Congo.

The day came when the four-man deputation was camped just a short distance from CT in Ibambi. The Rev Arthur Thynne, as leader of the deputation, took it upon himself to write to CT, to tell him they were a duly accredited deputation from the Home Committee and wanted to meet with him to discuss certain matters. He asked him for a time when they could visit and discuss things with him. One of the villagers was asked to deliver the letter by hand to CT. Within an hour a reply came from CT. As the Rev Thynne read the letter, he was devastated. It said:

> Since the Home Committee had been guilty of flagrant disobedience to his orders, he, as founder and head of the Mission, had dismissed them and had no intention of entering into any negotiations with them.[25]

No meeting ever took place. The deputation packed up and left Ibambi.

As the animosity between CT and the Home Committee increased, CT asked Norman and Pauline (Grubb) to return to the UK and present his situation to the Committee in person. They were the only family members who stayed close to CT during this period. Norman did not want to leave the Congo but agreed to do so.

The last meeting at which Norman Grubb heard *Bwana* speak was in 1931 at Imbai. A thousand people were packed into the church. Joy and expectation were on their faces. A withered old black woman full of the Holy Ghost led the prayer and there was wonderful singing. Then what the people were waiting for came. *Bwana* spoke for an hour on 'the pearl of great price'. He was too weak to stand and spoke seated on his chair. But that didn't matter to the people.

Once back in the UK, Norman and Pauline listened to what the Home Committee had to say. Norman's response was to try to help the Home Committee understand CT's 'unique qualities: his courage in an emergency, his determination never to sound the retreat, his conviction that he was in God's will, his faith that God would see him through, his contempt of the arm of flesh, and his willingness to risk all for Christ.'[26]

But the Home Committee did not want to listen and threatened to discipline and dismiss CT from the mission. Norman decided it was time to take drastic action. His mentor was Rees Howells, founder of the South Wales Bible College. Howells had encouraged him to reclaim the Mission in the name of the Lord, after noting in the mission's legal documents that the founder (C T Studd) had a veto and therefore the Committee couldn't kick him out.

The day after the Home Committee threatened to fire its founder, Norman and another brother-in-law, Colonel Munro, 'broke in' to the mission's headquarters at 17 Highland Road, to 'rescue' the records. The climax of the story is when Colonel Munro excitedly cut the phone lines in an act of bravery and defiance![27]

The Home Committee members resigned from WEC International and supported a new mission that Gilbert Buckley and Victor Evening started in Stanleyville in the Congo. It was called the 'Unevangelized Fields Mission' (today called 'Crossworld'). When it was formed in 1931, thirty-six missionaries serving with WEC International in the Congo and Brazil transferred across to it.

The work of WEC had to continue ... and it did. But six months later CT was promoted to glory. Norman Grubb described CT as the '*Moses of the mission*'. Moses led the nation of Israel out of slavery in Egypt into the wilderness. There for forty years he led with no compromise or backsliding, and was always at the forefront through the fiercest testings. He left behind an army of trained workers who had learnt his principles, stood with him through the trials, and knew how to go out and possess the Promised Land.

CHAPTER 13

The Final Years

One Last Visit Together (1928)

In CT's final years, despite age and ill health, nothing would stop him in his commitment to share the good news. As his body struggled with severe fever, heart attacks and continual bad indigestion, he reduced his visits to outlying areas and concentrated on leaving the written Word of God for the people. CT might not have written many books, but he was good at keeping in touch with his fellow missionaries by letter. He often ended the letters with 'your loving old father, CTS.'

Considerable work had been done for those in the Uele Province. Translation of God's Word into the Bangala language had proceeded as planned, with the majority of the work done by Alfred Buxton. In the Ituri province, however, little had been done and CT saw it as his responsibility to get on with it. By now nearly seventy, he still set to work, literarily working day and night. 'My days,' he wrote, 'are eighteen hours as a rule and no meals but what I gulp down as I write.'

CT only bothered with a plateful of food every few hours. Sometimes at the end of day his neck was so stiff through hours being bent over the table that he could not straighten up until Jack Harrison came and gently massaged it for him.

In 1926, he said: 'I've nearly completed Galatians. Praise God. Romans to Revelation finished.'[1] The translation of the New Testament into Kingwana was completed and it was published by the Scripture Gift Mission. CT then went on to also translate Psalms and parts of Proverbs.

Despite the pain and the tensions beneath the surface, nothing stopped him in his service for God. He was renowned as a workaholic – a 'Holy Ghost' inspired workaholic. A verse that summed up his life was: 'The zeal of thine house has eaten me up' (Psalm 69:9). In a thirteen-year period he was never known to have had a day off. He took no more than four hours of sleep in a twenty-four hour period.

In February 1928, when Priscilla visited her husband in the Congo for what would be the last time, her brief visit lasted only thirteen days. That was all the time she spent with CT in the last thirteen years of their married life. Norman Grubb who was there, described the visit:

> In 1928 his beloved wife, whom he had not seen in twelve
> years, and whom he had only been with for about two
> years since 1910, when he left for Africa, ... was travelling
> with a friend through the Mediterranean and landed in
> Egypt ... With the opening of roads, it was realised that
> she could reach CT in days, after leaving Rejaf on the Nile.

CT refused to travel to Egypt, so it was agreed for Priscilla to travel to see CT and the work in the Congo. Both knew, even before they met, that it would be their last meeting this side of heaven. [2]

Despite the brevity of the visit, the local Christians fell in love with Priscilla, whom they called *Mama Bwana*. CT later wrote of her visit that:

> She came. Once again I marvelled at the way God used her to speak to the natives. She seemed to know all about them and to speak to their very hearts. I have reason to know that few, if any, ever forgot her words. It was a joy to be on the same platform with her again. But her presence was an agony to me all the time. Plainly I could see the terrible cost to her of every day, yea hour, that she spent here.
>
> She pleaded with me to be allowed to stay. She almost became rebellious, and then how she prayed that I would go home with her, and assured me that the work would go on just the same here. There is never any doubt in one's mind when the real word of command from God comes. That command came to me, and it was 'Stay.'
>
> And so it was that we parted.[3]

That final parting was terrible. They knew it was the last time they would be together on earth and so said good bye to each other in CT's bamboo house before walking silently out to the waiting motor car. Priscilla got in with a set face and eyes straight ahead and was driven away. Victor Evening was one of the missionaries serving with WEC at the time of Priscilla's visit. He says that she told the Mission team before she left that she was going home a broken-hearted woman, and 'never spoke again at a Mission meeting, though everyone was looking forward to hearing a glowing account of her experiences in the Congo'[4].

A year later, the couple's daughter, Pauline, wrote to CT to tell him that on the 29 January 1929, aged 64, his beloved wife, after one day or sickness, was called home to be with the Lord. She had been visiting Malaga in Spain with a friend, Mrs Heber Radcliffe.[5]

> 'And so it was that we parted,' wrote CT.' I can only be
> thankful to God that He was gracious enough to take her
> to Himself without letting her go through what would
> have been so terrible to her, a long illness compelling her
> to inactivity.'[6]

On hearing the news of her death, his good friend and fellow Cambridge Seven member, Stanley Smith wrote to him from China, reminiscing about happy times together:

> My dear old Charlie, A few days ago I got a letter from
> Barclay Buxton, in which he told me that Scilla had 'fallen
> asleep' in Spain, where she had gone for rest. It is inspiring
> to think of her wholeheartedness, zeal and courage in the
> Lord's cause, but you, dear old man, and the mission, have
> lost a rare and true helpmeet. You have had the great gift of
> a truly devoted wife, and both of you put the Lord before
> each other. My mind goes back to your illness in Taiyuen,
> when you first told me about her.
>
> I have been looking up some old diaries about her. It
> was while I was at Luan looking for a house that she and
> Miss Burroughs passed through Taiyuen and went on to
> Hwochow. Here's some entries from these old diaries.

December 21st, 1887 – Got to Taiyuen (from Luan) about 10 o'clock; went to Tung chia hsiang, where to my intense joy I saw my dear Charlie Studd, looking so well. Praise the Lord!

January 5th, 1888 – Pressed on to Hwochow, walking about 110 miles. Got there after dark. Found Charlie with the ladies having a meeting. Hallelujah, Miss Stewart nearly well! I was deeply grateful to God for giving Miss Stewart to Charlie, and seeing her; she is indeed all Charlie says she is.

January 7th – Breakfast late-ish. Charlie's meals are all 'movable feasts'! A delightful meeting in Miss Stewart's room for prayer and praise.

January 8th – Outside service, it lasted for about three hours and a half, and they still wanted more – in some ways the finest native meeting I have been to in China.

January 9th – Praise meeting in Miss Stewart's room before going. Got to Hungtung not far off midnight.

May 16th – Early, a little after five o'clock in the morning, dear Charlie turned up with Mrs C T and Miss Burroughs. They had a very trying journey with a driver, as it were, possessed with the devil. It was such an intense joy, their coming – praise and glory be to God! Well, I need not pursue the subject further except to say I well know the self-denial exercised by you both in the opium refugee work before you went home (to the UK) in 1894.

October 10th – In morning up early; a long time again getting the things straight ... Got to Man-liukou well on in the afternoon; had some talk with Charlie, then prayer after we all had had food. Just about sunset they began to go on. Miss Bewes decided to go back, so she, Liu, T'ien, and myself returned, and Charlie, Scilla, 'nippers' Chi-fah, Teh hsin, and T-p'uh went on. The last words you said to me were, 'Hope to be back in a year's time'; but it was not to be![7]

Only One Life, 'Twill Soon be Past

In 1930, just one year before he died, CT was made *a Chevalier of the Royal Order of the Lion* by the King of the Belgians in recognition of his services to the Congo. He was too weak to go to Kinshasa to be presented with the medal and so it was delivered to him. The locals were thrilled with the award. It meant little to CT.

One of the native Christians that *Bwana* dearly loved was Adzangwe, a converted cannibal. CT made a visit to his village shortly before his death. At that time Adzangwe was also dying. He was suffering from consumption and the pallor could be seen beneath his black skin. All day, every day, Adzangwe lay on his bed in his little bamboo hut. To any who visited him to sympathise at his suffering, he would reply: 'You must not look sad when you come in here ... I am not sad. As I lie in bed I talk with God and He talks with me and Jesus Christ is round about me like the walls of this hut. I talk with *Bwana* also.'[8] (He had his photo pinned on the wall in front of his bed).

As soon as Adzangwe heard that *Bwana* had come to his village, nothing was going to keep him in his hut. He asked some of his neighbours if they would lift him into a chair and carry him over to the missionaries' house, where *Bwana* was sitting. By this stage CT was almost as weak and emaciated as Adzangwe.

Some of the missionaries carried a chair outside for *Bwana* to sit in. They placed some cushions on it to make it more comfortable for him. As he went to sit down, he took the cushions from the chair and placed them round the body of the converted cannibal. It was to be the last time the two men met on earth. They joked about being in a race to heaven and who might get there first. *Bwana* told Adzangwe that he was going to win and if he (Adzangwe) won, then he would have a row with him when they met up there! Three weeks later *Bwana* won the race.[9]

Knowing that his time on earth was near the end, CT wrote a letter home:

As I believe I am now nearing my departure from this world, I have but a few things to rejoice in; they are these:

1. That God called me to China and I went in spite of utmost opposition from all my loved ones.

2. That I joyfully acted as Christ told that rich young man to act.

3. That I deliberately at the call of God, when alone on the Bibby liner in 1910, gave up my life for this work, which was to be henceforth, not for the Sudan only, but for the whole unevangelized world.

My only joys therefore are that when God has given me a work to do, I have not refused it.[10]

CT's prayer was that he might die a soldier's death on the field of battle for Christ, and not be a burden to others for months and years as an invalid.

Sunday 12 July 1931, seemed like a normal day. CT conducted a five-hour service at Ibambi and told all the missionaries to go off to their different places of worship in the district, as they always did on the Lord's Day.

The next day, Monday, he asked for an injection of quinine because he felt cold and thought he might have a fever starting. By nightfall, the pain he was experiencing increased and was put down as gallstones. Jack Harrison stayed with him until 4 am. His condition worsened over the Tuesday and Wednesday.

By the Thursday CT was so weak that he could hardly speak. When one of the missionaries, asked him if he thought he was going to leave (the world), they thought he said: 'Very likely.' He ceased talking but occasionally words seemed to come from his mouth: 'Hallelujah! Hallelujah!'

As nightfall arrived CT slipped into unconsciousness. By 10.30 pm, still with a smile on his face, he was gone. Many years previously he had been asked what would happen to the Mission's work when he died. He replied quite simply: 'Then shall our mouths be filled with laughter. We will all shout Hallelujah. Our God will still be alive and nothing else matters.'[11]

Jack Harrison informed those at home in the UK of CT's death by cablegram.

Dear Old *Bwana* has gone to be with the Lord.
Let me assure you that through it all there has been the ring of victory, in *Bwana* himself, in the missionaries too, and more than all in the natives. Oh how we do praise

God for this … Hundreds of natives came at once and asked to see him. We had a 'lying in state' in the front room of *Bwana's* house. Hundreds filed passed the coffin and ever so reverently.

CT's death was put down to untreated gallstones.

On the day of his funeral, despite torrential rain, at his graveside gathered fifty missionaries and two thousand local Congolese, including a number of local chiefs. Those natives who had been close to him carried CT's coffin to the graveside where white missionaries lowered him into the grave. His coffin was draped in a specially designed Savita (Soldier-saint) flag that *Bwana* had designed. CT had requested the mood not to be solemn. The assembled crowd of mourners worshipped and lifted their voices in praise.

Back at his house after the funeral, the missionaries linked hands and sang:

> *Standing by the cross,*
> *Standing by the cross,*
> *We shall help each other,*
> *Standing by the cross.*

Those who had travelled in from outlying areas did not want to go home. On the Saturday special meetings were held. All present only seemed to have one thing on their minds – to rededicate themselves to God so the work *Bwana* had started could continue.

Amongst the many who paid tribute to him was his son-in-law, Alfred Buxton. He had, of course, travelled with him at the very beginning of the work in Africa … and then been summarily dismissed from the mission. He wrote:

Charles's life stands as some rugged Gibraltar – a sign to all succeeding generations that it is worthwhile to lose all this world can offer and stake everything on the world to come. His life will be an eternal rebuke to easy-going Christianity. He has demonstrated what it means to follow Christ without counting the cost or without looking back.

I myself owe an enormous debt to him. From him I learned that God's ideal of saint is not a man primarily concerned with his own sanctification; God's saint is fifty per cent a soldier. So we and thousands more will continue to thank God for the soldier-life he lived and the soldier-death he died. [12]

Epilogue

Only One Life

CT's legacy is all around us, but it is perhaps best summed up in a poem that in some ways has become more famous than C T Studd himself. Poetry writing was one of CT's little-known abilities.

This particular poem is attributed to CT by most biographers, although there is no direct available link to when he wrote it. Someone has written on the internet that they did not know who the author C T Studd was but the words of the poem summed up their life.[1]

ONLY ONE LIFE

Two little lines I heard one day,
Traveling along life's busy way;
Bringing conviction to my heart,
And from my mind would not depart;
Only one life, twill soon be past,
Only what's done for Christ will last.

NO SACRIFICE TOO GREAT

Only one life, yes only one,
Soon will its fleeting hours be done;
Then, in 'that day' my Lord to meet,
And stand before His Judgement seat;
Only one life, 'twill soon be past,
Only what's done for Christ will last.

Only one life, the still small voice,
Gently pleads for a better choice
Bidding me selfish aims to leave,
And to God's holy will to cleave;
Only one life, 'twill soon be past,
Only what's done for Christ will last.

Only one life, a few brief years,
Each with its burdens, hopes, and fears;
Each with its clays, I must fulfil,
living for self or in His will;
Only one life, 'twill soon be past,
Only what's done for Christ will last.

When this bright world would tempt me sore,
When Satan would a victory score;
When self would seek to have its way,
Then help me Lord with joy to say;
Only one life, 'twill soon be past,
Only what's done for Christ will last.

Give me Father, a purpose deep,
In joy or sorrow Thy word to keep;
Faithful and true what e'er the strife,
Pleasing Thee in my daily life;

Only one life, 'twill soon be past,
Only what's done for Christ will last.

Oh let my love with fervour burn,
And from the world now let me turn;
Living for Thee, and Thee alone,
Bringing Thee pleasure on Thy throne;
Only one life, 'twill soon be past,
Only what's done for Christ will last.

Only one life, yes only one,
Now let me say, 'Thy will be done';
And when at last I'll hear the call,
I know I'll say 'twas worth it all';
Only one life, 'twill soon be past,
Only what's done for Christ will last.'

(extra stanza)
Only one life, 'twill soon be past,
Only what's done for Christ will last.
And when I am dying, how happy I'll be,
If the lamp of my life has been burned out for Thee.

Unto the Uttermost Parts – WEC International

Long before C T Studd died, the international vision of the
Mission had already started. Although he never travelled beyond
his beloved Africa, others did, under the banner of WEC
International.

In 1922 the first WEC missionaries departed for the Amazon
to head a Mission work there. Wherever missionaries went, it had

been agreed that they would carry local names, as well as being part of WEC International. So, as Africa was still called by the name of Heart of Africa mission, so the work in the Amazon was referred to by the name of the Heart of the Amazonia mission.

The work in the Amazon was amongst the Red Indians. It was every bit as difficult as CT had experienced in the Congo. One of the first three missionaries, Fenton Hall, lost his life reaching out to the Guajajara tribe. Immediately three young Australians offered themselves for the work to fill the gap.

Kenneth Grubb and Harold Morris began a work amongst the Parentintin tribe, 1,200 miles up the Amazon. They faced torture and near death by starvation to bring the gospel to the tribe. By the time CT died in 1931, there was a staff team of sixteen missionaries working in the Amazon. Today the work is independent but still has workers in the region.

Jock Purves and Rex Bavington felt called to work in central Asia, in an area beyond the northern frontier of India. The Home Mission believed their call was genuine and sent them out. They crossed through mountainous terrain to work in an area called Little Tibet.

A fourth and fifth advance was made into Arabia and West Africa. The work had truly begun.

Even so, because of the tensions during CT's final years, the Mission he had started was struggling to survive at the time of his death. The leadership in the UK was taken on by his son-in-law, Norman Grubb and his wife, Pauline. It had been the original intention that Norman would take over leadership in the Congo but CT anointed Jack Harrison to that role when Norman returned following his discussions with the Home Committee. CT had been annoyed that, although Norman agreed with him regarding what he was saying to the Home Committee, he had objected to the way he was doing it.

Norman and Pauline were the sole representatives of the Mission in the UK at the time of CT's death. Assisting them were Daisy Kingdon, from the Congo, who had stood loyally by CT, and Elsie Dexter, the fiancé of one of the Congo missionaries.

However you looked at it, the Mission faced a crisis to survive:

- The founders had been called home to the Lord.
- No-one remained working in the Mission who was known to the general public.
- The Home Committee was not functioning.
- The UK was in a time of financial depression.
- There were thirty-five workers in the field, but the total support that came in for them in the first month after CT's death was £50.00.[2]

Norman, Pauline, Daisy and Elsie met every morning to find out what God planned for the future of the work. They sensed the Lord asked them what the original commission given to the founders was. They knew the answer was 'to evangelise the world.' The next question was: 'Well, are you going to do it?'

Norman and Pauline were aware that many obstacles faced them if they were to continue the work. But they also knew that when in the Bible people were asked to do the impossible, the only way it was done was *by faith*. The only memorial worthy of CT and Priscilla, was not one of stone or glass, but the Mission moving forward. They put out a fleece as a test of faith. 'Lord, if you are calling us to evangelise the world, we need to start by sending out reinforcements to the Congo.'

They told the Lord they did not just want to maintain the existing Mission work, they wanted twenty-five new workers and the funds (about £3,000) to send them to the mission field. They went on to ask for ten of the workers to be provided by the first anniversary of CT's death. Then for the other fifteen new workers in the second year. The verse of Scripture they took as their key verse was Mark 11:24: 'Whatever things you ask when you pray, believe that you receive them, and you will have them.'

Often when we desire something, we think we must keep praying until it happens. When the four in the Home office began praying again the second day for the new workers and finance, they immediately sensed the Spirit checked them and told them to stop asking, and start thanking … and that is what they did.

They covenanted with the Lord that no appeals would be made for more workers or for finances. Instead they would solely depend on the Lord and faith. They personally took a further costly step which set a pattern for development in the home countries. Conscious that every penny donated to the work would be quickly used up on the expanding fields, they took a stand of faith that, as Home staff, they would not accept a share of Mission gifts, but trust God for all their needs, accepting only gifts specifically earmarked for their personal use.[3]

They worked very hard. They used the leadership skills God had given them and they walked in faith for growth. As they studied the Scriptures they saw that part of walking in faith for people in the Bible was declaring beforehand what was going to be done, in assurance that it would be the case.

They acted on that by initially telling their own inner circle that God was going to send ten new workers during the summer. Then they wrote to those on the Mission field to tell them to prepare for the new workers, and finally they published it in the magazine.

Their faith was tested with the tenth worker they had asked for. He only applied to join the Mission ten days before the first anniversary of CT's death. They shared with the Mission supporters the story of the ten and their faith for a further fifteen. 'God has sent ten in one year, and we believe that he will send the other fifteen in the next year.'[4]

During the first five months of the second year, not a single application to join the Mission was received. It seemed that it would be impossible for fifteen to come forward during the second half of the year.

As they pondered on what was happening the Lord began to reveal to them His full plan for the mission. The name of the Mission had already been changed from Heart of Africa to the Worldwide Evangelization Crusade. In their minds however, Africa was still the thrust of the Mission and especially the Congo.

During the first half of the year, they had received applications from Christians to work in Colombia, South America, Arabia, Kashmir, (then northern India and today part-ruled by India and part by Pakistan) and Spanish Guinea in West Africa. Because of where the workers wanted to work, they had not seriously considered them. It gradually dawned on them what God was saying. *They were no longer a mission just to the Congo and Africa, but to the uttermost parts of the world.*

Of the fifteen who were recruited in the second year, two went to Colombia, two to Spanish Guinea, three to the Kashmir and one to the Congo. With six weeks left before the second anniversary of CT's death, there were still two vacancies for the full complement of fifteen, and about £500 needed.

On 15 June 1933 two more fully trained young men received the call to Colombia, and were accepted by the Mission. The required £500 came in from six different sources who knew nothing of the others who were giving.

Having proved God for twenty-five new workers over the first two years after CT's death, they felt the challenge to believe God for a further twenty-five new workers by the third anniversary of CT's death, and an extra sum of £3,250 to send them to the field.

In the fourth year, their faith challenge was increased to fifty new workers and an increase of £5,000. And that's exactly what happened. But maybe the story of how it happened and many other amazing examples of faith is the story for another book.

The same growth was seen on the mission field. There were those who said that the work in the Congo was built on *Bwana's* personality. Others said it was his gifting and skill in preaching and teaching and drawing in the net. Many wondered, as he departed this earth, what would happen to the work. Would it die – like him?

The opposite was the case. Collapse – No! Retreating and consolidation – Never! The work continued to advance.

A year after his death a conference was held in the Congo. Thousands upon thousands travelled to be part of it. Some estimated the numbers at 8,000. Even if that was an exaggeration, it was far larger than anything seen during *Bwana's* life. A similar conference was held two years after his death, at which over 10,000 Africans were present. The coming together of tribes and culture who previously had clashed and been violent towards each other for centuries, was truly a miracle of the power of the Gospel.

Today WEC International[5] still espouses the radical spirit that its founder expressed and has become an international community of some 1,800 missionaries serving in fifty-one different countries. In the area that CT started, today stands a healthy church, over 100,000 strong, with literally thousands coming to the Lord every year.

The Mission continues to follow the principles laid down by C T and Priscilla Studd. 'By Faith' remains the key to fulfilling the worldwide commission God has given for World Evangelisation for Christ.

Important Dates

1807   • Robert Morrison, first English missionary to serve in China, arrives in the country.

25 December 1819 • CT's father, Edward Studd, is born in Bombay, India.

January 1846   • Edward Studd marries Henrietta Margaret Hudson.

1853   • Henrietta Margaret dies.

1856   • Edward Studd marries Dora (CT Studd's mother) in UK.

2 December 1860 • Charles Thomas Studd is born.

28 August 1864   • Priscilla Stewart (CT's wife) is born in Lisburn, N Ireland.

1865   • China Inland Mission is formed.

1866	• The Studd family's horse, Salamander, wins the Grand National, Aintree, Liverpool.
1871	• Another Studd horse, Despatch, comes second in the Grand National, Aintree, Liverpool.
March-June 1875	• Moody and Sankey's Great London Crusade takes place at Majesty's Opera House, London.
1877	• Edward Studd is converted at Moody and Sankey meeting. His sons, Kynaston, George and CT make commitments to Christ.
1879	• CT Studd becomes captain of Eton cricket team.
	• CT's father, Edward, dies.
	• CT begins studies at Trinity College, Cambridge.
1882	• CT becomes only second Englishman to score 1,000 runs and take 100 wickets in a season.
November 1882	• Moody and Sankey mission is held at University of Cambridge.
1882-83	• CT is a member of the England cricket team that tours Ceylon and Australia, winning the first Ashes series.

1883	• CT captains Cambridge cricket team and is voted best all-round cricketer in the country.
1 August 1883	• CIM missionary, Harold Schofield, lays dying of diphtheria, in China, praying for God to raise up Christian leaders from the universities of Britain to serve in China
November 1883	• CT's brother George seriously ill, which led to CT making recommitment of his life to Christ.
1884 Summer	• CT obtains university degree and joins Middlesex County Cricket Club.
1 November	• CT makes commitment to serve the Lord in China.
4 November	• CT is interviewed at CIM headquarters and accepted for service in China.
	• Two-month Farewell Tour of UK for CT and other Cambridge Seven members.
1885 5 February	• Cambridge Seven leave UK for China.
18 March	• Cambridge Seven arrive in Shanghai, China.
1887	• 100 new CIM recruits arrived in Shanghai, including Priscilla Stewart
January	• CT gives away his inheritance.

April	• CT's brother, George, arrives in Shanghai.
7 April 1888	• CT and Priscilla's wedding before the British Consul in Tientsin, China.
1889	• Birth of Studd's first daughter, Grace, in China.
1894	• CT and Priscilla, with children, depart China for UK – never to return
October 1896 – April 1898	• Charles goes on an eighteen-month preaching tour in the USA.
1900	• Studd family departs for India.
1906	• Studd girls are baptised as believers.
	• Ill-health forces the family to leave India and return to the UK.
1908	• CT sees sign in Liverpool 'Cannibals want Missionaries' and attends meeting.
15 December 1910	• CT departs from Liverpool, to visit Sudan, Africa.
1911	• CT is unwell for most of the summer.
1912	• Studd family purchases their first home – 17 Highland Road, London.
31 January 1913	• CT embarks on his second trip to Africa, this time with Alfred Buxton.
	• Heart of Africa Mission is officially launched.

- Priscilla becomes seriously ill after attending Keswick Convention.

1914

19 June
- First baptismal service in the Congo.

28 June
- Beginning of First World War.

December
- Alfred Buxton stays in the Congo whilst CT returns to the UK.

1916

24 July
- CT departs the UK for the Congo, never to return to the UK. Priscilla remains in the UK.

December
- Wedding of Alfred Buxton and Edith (Studd) in the Congo.

1919
- CT and Priscilla's daughter, Dorothy, and husband Gilbert Barclay join the Mission, with Gilbert becoming Home Overseer.

- The Mission name changes to Worldwide Evangelization Crusade.

- Pauline Studd, the youngest daughter, arrives in Congo with husband Norman Grubb.

- Alfred and Edith depart the Congo for the UK with their baby daughter, Susan.

1920
- USA base is officially launched after a visit by Priscilla and Alfred Buxton.

1921	• Alfred and Edith return to the Congo. They leave their children with Alfred Buxton's mother.
	• CT's new teeth arrive in the Congo with Mr Buck.
	• Missionary Training Colony launched in Upper Norwood, London.
1922	• First WEC missionaries in the Amazon are appointed.
	• WEC Councils are formed in Australia, New Zealand and USA.
1923	• A total of 40 WEC missionaries are now serving in the Congo.
1924	• First American missionaries arrive in Congo to serve with WEC but depart within a few weeks. Canada base commenced.
1926	• Priscilla remains in the UK. Work starts in India (little Tibet).
1927	• Alfred and Edith are sent to USA to smooth difficulties with USA office.
	• CT writes to Alfred and dismissed him from Mission.
February 1928	• Priscilla visits CT in the Congo for two weeks – the only time she visits Africa
January 1929	• Priscilla dies in Malaga, Spain.

	• Norman and Pauline Grubb are sent to the UK.
1930	• The Belgian King decorates CT with Royal Order of the Lion.
1931 16 July	• CT Studd dies.
	• Norman Grubb is appointed General Secretary of the work.
July 1932	• Ten new workers join WEC.
July 1933	• Fifteen new workers join WEC.
July 1934	• Priscilla remains in the UK.
	• Twenty-five new workers join WEC.
July 1935	• Fifty new workers join WEC.
1982	• Name changes to Worldwide Evangelization for Christ (WEC) International
2021	• 1,800 workers serving in fifty-one countries with WEC International.

Who's Who

STUDD, Charles Thomas: (b 2 December 1860, d 16 July 1931). Referred to as *CT* and by the Africans as *Bwana*.

STUDD, Priscilla: (b 28 August 1864, d 15 January 1929). Married CT in April 1888 in China. Referred to by her nickname of *Scilla* by CT.

BEAUHere's some entries from these old diaries.**HAMP, (Rev Sir) Montagu**: (b 19 April 1850, d 26 October 1939). Member of the Cambridge Seven who went to China with C T. Went on to be a military chaplain during the First World War serving in Egypt, Greece, Murmansk.

BARNARDO, Thomas John: (b 4 July 1845, d 19 September 1905). Converted in 1862. Started orphanage work and Dr Barnardo's Homes.

BUXTON, Alfred: (b 3 November 1891, d 14 October 1940). Married CT and Priscilla's daughter, Edith, and pioneered the work in the Belgian Congo with CT.

CASSELS, Rev William Wharton: (b 11 March 1858, d 7 November 1925). Studied at St John's College, Cambridge. Member of the Cambridge Seven who went to China with CT. In 1895, he became the Bishop of Western China (Hua Hsi Diocese). He was considered one of the most forward missionaries of his time.

GRUBB, Norman: (b 2 August 1895, d 15 December 1993). Married CT and Priscilla's daughter, Pauline, and took responsibility for the work of WEC International following the deaths of CT and Priscilla.

GRUNNE, Count de: (b unknown, d unknown). Member of Roman Catholic Church and Commissioner in the Belgian 'Dungu' region. He greatly helped CT and Alfred as they established the Mission in the Congo.

Hoste, Mr Dixon E: (b 23 July 1861, d 11 May 1946). Member of the Cambridge Seven who went to China with CT. He served in the Royal Artillery and never attended Cambridge University. He became the successor to Hudson Taylor as General Director of the China Inland Mission (1902-1935).

HSI, Pastor: (b around 1836 in Shanxi, d not known but thought to be around 1896). Former opium addict, wonderfully converted. He became a pastor and evangelist. He married CT and Priscilla in China and worked with them in their opium clinic in Lungan-Fu.

KUMM, (Dr) Karl: (b 25 November 1862, d 15 August 1946). Founder of Sudan United Mission. He advertised a meeting in Liverpool with sign 'Cannibals want Missionary', which resulted in CT's call to Africa.

MEYER, F B: (b 8 April 1847, d 28 March 1929). Baptist minister at York, Leicester, Regents Park London and Christ Church Chapel, Westminster. He was a prolific writer and Keswick Convention speaker. He was greatly influenced by CT and remained friends with him throughout his life.

MOODY, Dwight Lyman: (b 5 February 1837, d 22 December 1899). With soloist Ira Sankey, possible the greatest evangelists of the nineteenth century. In 1882, at the invitation of Kynaston Studd, he held a mission at Cambridge University, which was a prelude to the sending out of the Cambridge Seven to China.

MOTT, John Raleigh: (b 25 May 1865, d 31 January 1955). Challenged in his faith through hearing Kynaston Studd speak in the USA. He went on to be an influential figure in mission as Chairman of the Student Volunteer Movement. He was awarded the Nobel Committee Peace Prize in 1946.

MÜLLER, George: (b 27 September 1805, d 10 March 1898). Born in Prussia, he pastored churches in Teignmouth and Bristol. During his time in Bristol he cared for over 10,000 orphans and began 117 'Christian' schools.

POLHILL-TURNER, Arthur: (b 7 February 1862, d 21 November 1935). Member of the Cambridge Seven who went to China with CT, and stayed there for most of the next forty-three years.

POLHILL-TURNER, Cecil: (b 23 February 1860, d 9 March 1938). Member of the 2nd Dragoon Guards, who never went to

Cambridge University. He became a member of the Cambridge Seven and went to China with CT, staying there until the Boxer Uprising of 1900.

RADSTOCK, Lord and 3rd Baron: (b 10 April 1833, d 8 December 1913). Family friend of CT and Priscilla. He had a spiritual experience whilst involved in the Crimean War and undertook missionary work in Russia. He was a member of George Müller's church in Bristol.

SMITH, Stanley: (b 19 March 1861, d 31 January 1931). Member of the Cambridge Seven and went to China with CT. He remained close friends with CT and Priscilla all his life. In the late 1890s he resigned from the China Inland Mission over a doctrinal issue and remained in China as an independent missionary until his death.

STUDD, Dora Sophie: (b 11 May 1833, d 20 March 1923). Mother of CT and second wife of Edward.

STUDD, Dorothy: (b 9 July 1891, d 2 November 1980). Daughter of CT and Priscilla. She married Rev Gilbert Barclay. They had six children and she became involved in WEC International in the UK.

STUDD, Edith: (b 23 September 1892, d 10 September 1977). Daughter of CT and Priscilla Studd. She married Alfred Buxton in the Congo. She pioneered the work in the Belgian Congo with both her husband and her father.

STUDD, Edward: (b 25 December 1819, d 27 July 1877). Father of CT. He was a retired wealthy Indian jute and indigo plantation owner.

STUDD, George: (b 20 October 1859, d 13 February 1945). Brother of CT. He became seriously ill, which resulted in CT's recommitment to faith in Christ. He joined the Apostolic Faith Mission in 1907 and worked in difficult areas in Los Angeles, California.

STUDD, Grace: (b 13 February 1889, d 2 January 1974). Eldest daughter of CT and Priscilla. She was married twice.

STUDD, (Sir) Kynaston: (b 26 July 1858, d 14 January 1944). Older brother of CT. He held various responsibilities including being Lord Mayor of London twice, President of the Royal Polytechnic Institute and President of the MCC.

STUDD, Pauline: (b 10 February 1894, d 1 September 1981). Daughter of CT and Priscilla. She married Norman Grubb, who took over the leadership of WEC International on CT's death.

VINCENT, Mr: (b unknown, d unknown). A retired Indian jute farmer, who took his friend Edward Studd (CT's father) to a Moody and Sankey meeting where Studd committed his life to Christ.

Bibliography

There are many books and articles about C T and Priscilla Studd. These are some of the books and articles I have used in my research, which I would recommend to you if you want to read further about CT and Priscilla.

Benge, Janet, and Benge, Geoff, *C T Studd – No Retreat, Christian Heroes: Then and Now* (Seattle: YWAM Publishing, 2005).

Bonk, J, 'Studd, C(harles) T(homas)' in Gerald H Anderson, ed, *Biographical Dictionary of Christian Missions* (New York: Macmillan Reference USA, 1998), 649.

Broomhall, A J, *Hudson Taylor and China's Open Century,* vi: *Assault on the Nile* (London: Hodder & Stoughton, 1990).

Broomhall, A J, *Hudson Taylor and China's Open Century,* vii: *It is not Death to Die* (London: Hodder & Stoughton, 1990).

Broomhall, Benjamin, *The Evangelism of the World: A Missionary Band: A Record of Consecration and an Appeal* (London: Morgan & Scott, 1989).

Broomhall, Ruth, *James Hudson Taylor: Called by God into the Heart of the Dragon* (Farnham: CWR, 2018).

Dinnen, Stewart, *Here We Stand* (London: China Inland Mission, 1984) (Smashwords edn, 2014).

Davies, Evan, *Whatever Happened to C T Studd's Mission? Lessons from the History of WEC International* (London: WEC Publications, 2012).

Erskine, John T, *Millionaire for God: The Story of C T Studd*, Stories of Faith and Fame (Cambridge: The Lutterworth Press, 1986).

Grubb, Norman P, *C T Studd, Cricketer and Pioneer* (Cambridge: The Lutterworth Press, 1933).

Grubb, Norman P, *C T Studd, Athlete and Pioneer* (London: United Society for Christian Literature (formerly Religious Tract Society), 1943).

Evening, Martin (ed), *Victor Evening, 'Studd's Mission, DCD'* (Milton Keynes: Lightning Sources UK (print on demand). Martin Evening shares his father's experiences serving with C T Studd in the Belgian Congo in the early 1920s.

Pollock, J C, *A Cambridge Movement* (London: John Murray, 1953). (Forward by Clifford Martin, The Lord Bishop of Liverpool).

BIBLIOGRAPHY

Pollock, John, *Moody Without Sankey: A Biography*, History Makers (rev edn, Fearn: Christian Focus Publications, 1995).

Pollock, John, *The* Cambridge Seven*: The True Story of Ordinary Men Used in no Ordinary Way*, History Makers (rev edn, Fearn: Christian Focus Publications, 2012).

Studd, C T, *Reminiscences of Mrs C T Studd*, [Kindle edn] (London: Real Good Books, 2014). C T Studd shares his memories of his wife from throughout their lives as they served in China, India, and Africa.

Vincent, Eileen, *C T Studd and Priscilla* (London: Kingsway Publications, 1988).

Endnotes

Preface

1   Gordon Pettie, Use Even Me, Lord (Sutton Coldfield, UK: Fines Creek
    Publishing, 2019).

2   J Hudson Taylor, ed, China's Millions, March 1885 edn (Toronto: China
    Inland Mission, 1885).

3   Buxton, Alfred, 'Foreword' in Norman R Grubb, C T Studd, Cricketer
    and Pioneer (Cambridge: The Lutterworth Press, 1933), 3.

4   George Verwer, Confessions of a Toxic Perfectionist and God's Antidote
    (np: OM Ships/Good Shepherd Books, 2020).

Introduction

1   Eileen Vincent, *C T Studd and Priscilla* (London: Kingsway Publications,
    1988), 229-30.

2   C T Studd, *Reminiscences of Mrs C T Studd*. [Kindle edn] (London: Real
    Good Books, 2014.

Chapter 1

1   Norman R Grubb, *C T Studd, Cricketer and Pioneer* (Cambridge: The
    Lutterworth Press, 1933), 12.

2   Grubb, *C T Studd, Cricketer and Pioneer*, 13.

3   J C Pollock, *A Cambridge Movement* (London: John Murray, 1953), 54-5.

4   Esthme Ethelind Enock, *Twelve Mighty Missionaries* (London, Pickering & Inglis, 1948), 75.

5   Grubb, *C T Studd, Cricketer and Pioneer*, 13.

6   Grubb, *C T Studd, Cricketer and Pioneer*, 14.

7   John Pollock, *Moody Without Sankey: A Biography*, History Makers (rev edn, Fearn: Christian Focus Publications, 1995), 186.

8   Grubb, *C T Studd, Cricketer and Pioneer*, 17.

9   Grubb, *C T Studd, Cricketer and Pioneer*, 17.

10 Pollock, *Moody Without Sankey,* 148.

11 Grubb, *C T Studd, Cricketer and Pioneer*, 18-19.

12 Vincent, *C T Studd and Priscilla,* 27.

13 Benge, Janet, and Benge, Geoff, *C T Studd – No Retreat, Christian Heroes: Then and Now* (Seattle: YWAM Publishing, 2005), 30.

Chapter 2

1   Eton v Harrow match report of 1879, quoted in Grubb, *C T Studd, Cricketer and Pioneer,* 22.

2   Grubb, *C T Studd, Cricketer and Pioneer,* 22.

3   Grubb, *C T Studd, Cricketer and Pioneer,* 23.

4   John Welford, 'C T Studd: A Cricketer Who Became a Missionary', *How They Play* (26 March 2020), http:// https://howtheyplay.com/team-sports/ C-T-Studd-A-Cricketer-Who-Became-A-Missionary, accessed 20 October 2021.

5   Arunabha Sengupta, 'The Miracle of the Studd Brothers: Cambridge University Beat the 1882 Australians', *Cricket Country* (9 September 2015), https://www.cricketcountry.com/news/the-miracle-of-the-studd-brothers-cambridge-university-beat-the-1882-australians-327441, accessed 20 October 2021.

6   Martin Evening (ed), *Victor Evening, 'Studd's Mission, DCD'* (Milton Keynes: Lightning Sources UK (print on demand), 8.

ENDNOTES

7   Sengupta, 'The Miracle of the Studd Brothers', *Cricket County* (9 September 2015), accessed 20 October 2021.

8   Sengupta, 'The Miracle of the Studd Brothers', *Cricket County* (9 September 2015), accessed 20 October 2021.

9   W G Grace found fame and fortune by hiring locums to look after his medical practice while he played first class cricket for a staggering 43 years.

10 Pollock, *A Cambridge Movement*, 74.

11 Welford, 'C T Studd: A Cricketer Who Became a Missionary', *How They Play* (26 March 2020), accessed 20 October 2021.

Chapter 3

1   Pollock, *A Cambridge Movement*, 55.

2   Broomhall, *Hudson Taylor and China's Open Century*, vi: *Assault on the Nile* (London: Hodder & Stoughton, 1990), 332.

3   Pollock, *A Cambridge Movement*, 58.

4   John Pollock, *The Cambridge Seven: The True Story of Ordinary Men Used in no Ordinary Way*, History Makers (rev edn, Fearn: Christian Focus Publications, 2012), 72.

5   Vincent, *C T Studd and Priscilla*, 33.

6   Grubb, *C T Studd, Cricketer and Pioneer*, 33.

7   Broomhall, *Hudson Taylor and China's Open Century*, Book 6, 340

8   Benge and Benge, *C T Studd*, 39.

9   In time Wilfred Grenfell served as a pioneer doctor in Labrador, today part of Canada. By the time of his retirement in 1932, largely through Grenfell's drive, Labrador had six hospitals, four hospital ships, seven nursing stations, two orphanages, two large schools, fourteen industrial centres and a co-operative lumber mill. King George V knighted him in 1927 for his services to Labrador, Canada.Sir Wilfred Grenfell, *Forty Years for Labrador*, (London: Hodder and Stoughton, 1934), 35.

10 Grubb, *C T Studd, Cricketer and Pioneer*, 34.

11 A leading figure in the Holiness Movement in the United States and the Higher Life Movement in the United Kingdom. Also active in the Women Suffrage and Temperance Movements

12   Vincent, *C T Studd and Priscilla*, 41.

13   Pollock, *The Cambridge Seven*, 68.

Chapter 4

1   In time he was to remarry and return to China where he served for
     another 33 years. When he died in 1904, the *China Inland Mission* had
     205 Mission stations, 800 missionaries and 125,000 new believers were
     attached to the mission.

2   Pollock, *The Cambridge Seven*, 44.

3   Pollock, *The Cambridge Seven*, 44.

4   Pollock, *The Cambridge Seven*, 44-5.

5   David Joannes, *The Mind of a Missionary: C T Studd* (Prescott, AZ:
     Within Reach Global Inc, 2018). quoting from Geraldine Guinness,
     The Story of the China Inland Mission (London: Morgan & Scott, 1894),
     Chapter XXIX.
     God answered his prayers through C T Studd and the Cambridge Seven.

6   Broomhall, *Hudson Taylor and China's Open Century*, Book 6, 316-7.

7   In May 1885 C T Studd reached Taiyuan, the capital of Shanxi Province,
     and managed to find his way to the house that Dr Harold Schofield's had
     made his home, surgery and prayer closet. As he stood there, with Hudson
     Taylor, he knew that he and other members of the *Cambridge Seven* were
     the living answer to his prayer. He had prayed. They were the answer.

8   1 Corinthians 1: 26 – 29.

9   Marshall Broomhall, *By Love Compelled: The Call of the China Inland
     Mission* (London: Hodder & Stoughton, 1936), 37.

10   Pollock, *The Cambridge Seven*, 18.

11   Pollock, *The Cambridge Seven*, 24.

12   Pollock, *The Cambridge Seven*, 76.

13   Pollock, *The Cambridge Seven*, 57.

14   Pollock, *The Cambridge Seven*, 60.

15   Pollock, *The Cambridge Seven*, 13.

16   Pollock, *The Cambridge Seven*, 34.

17   Pollock, *The Cambridge Seven*, 45.

ENDNOTES

18   Pollock, *The Cambridge Seven*, 89.

19   J Hudson Taylor, ed, *China's* Millions, March

20   Pollock, *The Cambridge Seven*, 70-1.

21   Grubb, *C T Studd, Cricketer and Pioneer*, 38.

22   Pollock, *The Cambridge Seven*, 71.

23   Broomhall, *Hudson Taylor and China's Open Century*, Book 6, 341.

24   Broomhall, *Hudson Taylor and China's Open Century*, Book 6, 377.

Chapter 5

1   Grubb, *C T Studd, Cricketer and Pioneer*, 45.

2   J C Pollock: *The Keswick Story: The Authorised History of the Keswick Movement* (London: Hodder& Stoughton, 1964).

3   Vincent, *C T Studd and Priscilla*, 56.

4   Broomhall, *Hudson Taylor and China's Open Century*, Book 6, 358.
     Broomhall, *Hudson Taylor and China's Open Century*, Book 6, 341.

5   Grubb, *C T Studd, Cricketer and Pioneer*, 43.

6   Pollock, *The Cambridge Seven*, 89.

7   Pollock, *The Cambridge Seven*, 89.

8   Grubb, *C T Studd, Cricketer and Pioneer*, 44.

9   Pollock, *The Cambridge Seven*, 92.

10   Benge and Benge, *C T Studd*, 45.

11   Grubb, *C T Studd, Cricketer and Pioneer*, 45.

12   Broomhall, *Hudson Taylor and China's Open Century*, Book 6, 358.

13   Mrs Howard Taylor, *Faith's Ventures: A Shorter Life of Hudson Taylor* (London: China Inland Mission, 1960), 145.

14   Pollock, *The Cambridge Seven*, 95.

15   Grubb, *C T Studd, Cricketer and Pioneer*, 47.

16   Pollock, *The Cambridge Seven*, 102.

17   Broomhall, *Hudson Taylor and China's Open Century*, Book 6, 363.

18   Summary of qualification listed in J Hudson Taylor, ed, *China's* Millions, March 1885 edn.

Chapter 6

1   Broomhall, *Hudson Taylor and China's Open Century*, Book 6, 364.

2   Vincent, *C T Studd and Priscilla*, 63.

3   Vincent, *C T Studd and Priscilla*, 64.

4   Grubb, *C T Studd, Cricketer and Pioneer*, 53-4, 54, 55.

5   Broomhall, *Hudson Taylor and China's Open Century*, Book 6, 374.

6   Grubb, *C T Studd, Cricketer and Pioneer*, 56, 57.

7   Broomhall, *Hudson Taylor and China's Open Century*, Book 6, 375.

8   Grubb, *C T Studd, Cricketer and Pioneer*, 57-8.

9   Broomhall, *Hudson Taylor and China's Open Century*, Book 6, 375.

10   Dinnen, Stewart, *Here We Stand* (London: China Inland Mission, 1984) (Smashwords edn, 2014), 295-8.

11   Studd, *Reminiscences of Mrs C T Studd*.

12   Studd, *Reminiscences of Mrs C T Studd*.

13   Grubb, *C T Studd, Cricketer and Pioneer*, 75.

Chapter 7

1   Grubb, *C T Studd, Cricketer and Pioneer*, 67.

2   Grubb, *C T Studd, Cricketer and Pioneer*, 68.

3   Grubb, *C T Studd, Cricketer and Pioneer*, 69, 70.

4   Studd, *Reminiscences of Mrs C T Studd*.

5   Studd, *Reminiscences of Mrs C T Studd*.

6   Grubb, *C T Studd, Cricketer and Pioneer*, 73.

7   Grubb, *C T Studd, Cricketer and Pioneer*, 73.

8   Studd, *Reminiscences of Mrs C T Studd*.

9   Studd, *Reminiscences of Mrs C T Studd*.

10   Studd, *Reminiscences of Mrs C T Studd*.

11   Studd, *Reminiscences of Mrs C T Studd*.

12   Grubb, *C T Studd, Cricketer and Pioneer*, 79-80.

13   Grubb, *C T Studd, Cricketer and Pioneer*, 83.

14   Papers provided by CIM/OMF, of notes written by Charles Studd, date unknown

15   Studd, *Reminiscences of Mrs C T Studd*.

16 John T Erskine, *Millionaire for God: The Story of C T Studd*, Stories of Faith and Fame (Cambridge: The Lutterworth Press, 1986), 31.

17 Grubb, *C T Studd, Cricketer and Pioneer*, 80.

18 Grubb, *C T Studd, Cricketer and Pioneer*, 80-1.

19 Papers provided by CIM/OMF of notes written by CT Studd, date unknown, 9.

20 Studd, *Reminiscences of Mrs C T Studd.*

21 Benge and Benge, *C T Studd*, 74.

22 Vincent, *C T Studd and Priscilla*, 78.

23 Studd, *Reminiscences of Mrs C T Studd.*

24 Vincent, *C T Studd and Priscilla*, 99.

25 Grubb, *C T Studd, Cricketer and Pioneer*, 92.

26 Studd, *Reminiscences of Mrs C T Studd.*

Chapter 8

1 Grubb, *C T Studd, Cricketer and Pioneer*, 95.

2 Quote contained in papers supplied by China Inland Mission/OMF, believed to be from personal memoirs of C T Studd.

3 Alex Bunn, 'Heroes 11: CT Studd (1860-1931): Not just cricket!', *Nucleus* (Christian Medical Fellowship Publication) (September 2013).

4 Pollock, *A Cambridge Movement*, 132.

5 Pollock, *A Cambridge Movement*, 143.

6 He also became the first Englishman to die flying in July 1910.

7 It is estimated that, by 1945, 25,000 students entered into Christian service as a result of the Student Volunteer Movement.
Evan Davies, *Whatever Happened to C T Studd's Mission? Lessons from the History of WEC International* (London: WEC Publications, 2012), 46.

8 Grubb, *C T Studd, Cricketer and Pioneer*, 106, 132, 133, 134.

9 Grubb, *C T Studd, Cricketer and Pioneer*, 109.

10 A quote by Charles's son in law, Mr Buxton, according to Enock, *Twelve Mighty Missionaries.*

11 Grubb, *C T Studd, Cricketer and Pioneer*, 111, 112.

12 Grubb, *C T Studd, Cricketer and Pioneer*, 111.

Chapter 9

1   Bunn, Heroes 11: CT Studd (1860-1931): Not just cricket!', *Nucleus*, (CMF) (September 2013).

2   Grubb, *C T Studd, Cricketer and Pioneer,* 116.

3   A 'growler' was built to work as a cab on city streets, 'growling' across the cobbles!

4   C T Studd, *The Chocolate Soldier* (Fort Washington, PA: Christian Literature Crusade. 1912. Also London: WEC Publications, 1989).

5   Evening, *Studd's Mission,* 27.

6   Vincent, *C T Studd and Priscilla,* 128.

7   Benge and Benge, *C T Studd,* 107.

8   Benge and Benge, *C T Studd,* 107.

9   Benge and Benge, *C T Studd,* 108.

10 Dinnen, Stewart, *Here We Stand,* 302-5.

11 Erskine, *Millionaire for God,* 47.

12 Grubb, *C T Studd, Cricketer and Pioneer,* 122.

13 Grubb, *C T Studd, Cricketer and Pioneer,* 123.

14 Benge and Benge, *C T Studd,* 111.

15 Grubb, *C T Studd, Cricketer and Pioneer,* 125.

16 A historical region of north-western South Sudan, named after the river of the same name.

17 Timothy Alford, 'C T Studd (1860-1931)', *Evangelical Times (November 2010).*

18 WEC Leaders Council, *Core of WEC,* https://www.wecinternational.org/admin/resources/core-of-wec.pdf, 2.

19 Davies, *Whatever Happened to C T Studd's Mission?,* 17.

20 Evening, *Studd's Mission,* 18, 21.

21 Studd, *Reminiscences of Mrs C T Studd.*

22 Grubb, *C T Studd, Cricketer and Pioneer,* 131-2.

23 Grubb, *C T Studd, Cricketer and Pioneer,* 131-2.

24 Grubb, *C T Studd, Cricketer and Pioneer,* 133.

25 Grubb, *C T Studd, Cricketer and Pioneer,* 133.

26 Benge and Benge, *C T Studd,* 124.

27 Erskine, *Millionaire for God*, 57.

28 Belgian colonisation of the Congo began in 1885 when King Leopold II founded and ruled the Congo Free State. Many outposts were built to extend his power over such a vast territory. Reports of widespread murder, torture and other abuses in the rubber plantations led to outrage, both internationally and in Belgium, and the Belgian Government transferred control of the region from Leopold II, (who claimed the land as his personal property) and established the Belgian Congo in 1908. The Congo became independent in 1960, after an uprising by the Congolese people.

29 Jean Walker. *Fool and Fanatic?: Quotations from the Letters of C T Studd.* (Gerrards Cross, Buckinghamshire: Worldwide Evangelization Crusade, 1980), quoted in Davies, *Whatever Happened to C T Studd's Mission?*, 73.

30 Grubb, *C T Studd, Cricketer and Pioneer*, 148.

31 Studd, *Reminiscences of Mrs C T Studd.*

Chapter 10

1 Grubb, *C T Studd, Cricketer and Pioneer*, 151.

2 The Northern Ireland Bible teacher, David Legge, told this story in 'The Twin Secrets of Haggai and Zecchariah's Success', *Preach the Word*, August 2010, https://www.preachtheword.com/sermon/misc0098-twin-secrets.shtml.

3 Grubb, *C T Studd, Cricketer and Pioneer*, 151-2.

4 Erskine, *Millionaire for God*, 55.

5 Studd, *Reminiscences of Mrs C T Studd.*

Chapter 11

1 Evening, *Studd's Mission*, 4.

2 Benge and Benge, *C T Studd*, 152.

3 Grubb, *C T Studd, Cricketer and Pioneer*, 161.

4 Benge and Benge, *C T Studd*, 153-4.

5 Evening, *Studd's Mission*, 3.

6 Benge and Benge, *C T Studd*, 161-2.

7 Benge and Benge, *C T Studd*, 155.

8 Grubb, *C T Studd, Cricketer and Athlete*, 162.

9 Benge and Benge, *C T Studd*, 166.

10 Grubb, *C T Studd, Cricketer and Pioneer*, 165.

11 Grubb, *C T Studd, Cricketer and Pioneer*, 169-70.

12 Grubb, *C T Studd, Cricketer and Pioneer*, 173.

13 Benge and Benge, *C T Studd*, 154-5.

14 Grubb, *C T Studd, Cricketer and Pioneer*, 171.

15 In 1922 WEC began working in the Amazon region in South America. By the time of CT's death in 1931 the Amazonian work had sixteen missionaries in three people groups. The work then grew into Central Asia, Arabia, West Africa, Columbia n iSouth America.

16 Grubb, *C T Studd, Cricketer and Pioneer*, 183.

17 Studd, *Reminiscences of Mrs C T Studd*.

Chapter 12

1 Grubb, *C T Studd, Cricketer and Pioneer*, 206.

2 Grubb, *C T Studd, Cricketer and Pioneer*, 207.

3 Grubb, *C T Studd, Cricketer and Pioneer*, 215.

4 Eileen Vincent, *No Sacrifice Too Great: The Story of C T and Priscilla Studd*, (2nd edn, Gerrards Cross, Buckinghamshire: Worldwide Evangelization Crusade, 1992), 206.

5 Norman Grubb says the College began in 1921. Wikipedia says it started in 1923. It is believed the Norman Grubb date is correct. The training college continues to this day as part of the All Nations Christian College, after a series of mergers.

6 Vincent, *No Sacrifice Too Great*, 207.

7 The sacraments were not restored to the WEC Churches for ten years, by which time CT had died, and Jack Harrison was the field leader. Davies, *Whatever Happened to C T Studd's Mission?*, 10.

8 Dinnen, *Here We Stand*, 471-5

9 Davies, *Whatever happened to C T Studd's mission?*

10 Vincent, *C T Studd and Priscilla*, 225.

11 Buxton and some other former Congolese missionaries went on to link with T A Lambie and the Sudan Interior Mission, to open new work in Ethiopia and Somalia. He and his brother Murray died when they were attending a committee meeting at the Church House, Westminster in 1940 and it was struck in an air raid. Gerard H Anderson (Ed) *Biographical Dictionary of Christian Missions,* (Grand Rapids, Michigan:William Eerdmans Publishing, 1999).

12 Vincent, *C T Studd and Priscilla,* 224.

13 Grubb, *C T Studd, Cricketer and Pioneer,* 180.

14 Vincent, *C T Studd and Priscilla,* 224.

15 Evening, *Studd's Mission,* 235.

16 Grubb, *C T Studd, Cricketer and Pioneer.*

17 Evening, *Studd's Mission,* 195.

18 Evening, *Studd's Mission,* 196.

19 Studd, *The Chocolate Soldier,* 24.

20 Studd, *The Chocolate Soldier,* 4.

21 Davies, *Whatever Happened to C T Studd's Mission?,* 27.

22 Vincent, *C T Studd and Priscilla,* 229-30.

23 Vincent, *C T Studd and Priscilla,* 230.

24 Vincent, *C T Studd and Priscilla.*

25 Evening, *Studd's Mission,* 258.

26 Norman P Grubb, *C T Studd, Athlete and Pioneer* (London: United Society for Christian Literature (formerly Religious Tract Society), 1943), 6.

27 Joanna Coatney, 'A Review of CT Studd in the Heart of Africa by Norman Grubb', *The* Intercessor, Vol 26/1 (Zerubbabel Ministries, January 2010).

Chapter 13

1 Vincent, *C T Studd and Priscilla,* 231.

2 Grubb, *C T Studd, Cricketer and Pioneer,* 219.

3 Studd, *Reminiscences of Mrs C T Studd.*

4 Evening, *Studd's Mission,* 210.

5 Grubb, *C T Studd, Cricketer and Pioneer,* 219.

6 Studd, *Reminiscences of Mrs C T Studd,* 132.

7   Studd, *Reminiscences of Mrs C T Studd*.

8   Grubb, *C T Studd, Cricketer and Pioneer*, 221.

9   Grubb, *C T Studd, Cricketer and Pioneer*, 223.

10   *Thomas John Bach, Pioneer Missionaries for Christ and His Church (Wheaton, Ill: Van Kampen Press, 1955)*.

11   Enock, *Twelve Mighty Missionaries*, 80.

12   Vincent, *C T Studd and Priscilla*, 234.

Epilogue

1   The poem inspired the song 'Only one Life' written by Lanny Wolfe in 1973.

2   Norman Grubb, *The Intercessor*, Vol 2/1 (Zerubbabel Ministries, January 1986).

3   Dinnen, *Here We Stand*, 80-3.

4   Grubb, *C T Studd, Cricketer and Pioneer*, 230-1.

5   Recognising some misunderstandings with using the word 'crusade', the Mission was renamed as Worldwide Evangelisation for Christ (WEC International).

OTHER BOOKS BY GORDON PETTIE

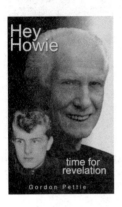

A new kind of Christian television station was launched in the United Kingdom on February 14th 2003 – Revelation TV. Its founder, Howard Conder, had lived the dream for the early part of his life. He played in the pop groups of his day - the Baron Knights, and Joe Brown and the Bruvvers. He mixed with the likes of Bob Marley, David Bowie and even played on the same billing as the Beatles on one occasion. But despite the glamour and the wealth, there was a hunger for something more. Howard left the UK with his family for the United States. It was there he discovered Christ.

Fast forward many years and the Lord called Howard to give up the successful music studio he was running in Florida and move back to Britain and start a Christian television station.

This is the story of Howard Conder and Revelation TV. Read the full story in **HEY HOWIE** by Gordon Pettie

Revelation TV broadcasts 24 hours a day, every day, on Sky 581, Freesat 692 and many other places.

To order copies of this book please contact the Revelation TV office on +44 208 972 1400 or by emailing to infor@revelationtv.com

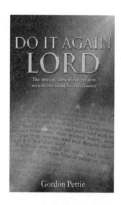

Do It Again Lord contains the story of six of the greatest revivals in church history. Scholars agree that if the Welsh revival of 1904 and the Azusa Street revival of 1906 had taken place during the first century, we would likely read about them today in the Bible, in the Acts of the Apostles.

What is revival? Discover the history of what happened in these six revivals and learn revival principles, as you read the stories of the 1904 Welsh revival with Evan Roberts, the 1906 Azusa Street revival with William Seymour, along with the revival in America in 1857, Ulster in 1859, Korea (yes, Korea – especially north Korea) in 1907, and the Isle of Lewis in the Hebrides in 1949 with Duncan Campbell.

Alistair Cole, then Chairman of the Elim Prayer Network and now Director of The Watchman Ministry, has written of this book, *"Quite one of the best books on the subject of revival I have ever read. My prayer is DO IT AGAIN, LORD".*

"There are important lessons to learn from each revival. My longing is that your life will be impacted as you learn them" - Gordon Pettie

To order copies of this book please contact the Revelation TV office on +44 208 972 1400 or by emailing to infor@revelationtv.com

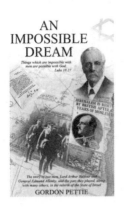

AN IMPOSSIBLE DREAM

Things which are impossible with men are possible with God.
Luke 18.27

The story of two men, Lord Arthur Balfour and General Edmund Allenby, and the part they played, along with many others, in the rebirth of the State of Israel

GORDON PETTIE

On the 14th May 1948 the State of Israel was established. '**An Impossible Dream**' looks at the historical steps that God put in place in the early part of the twentieth century to make the United Nations resolution concerning the state of Israel a reality. Although the Jewish people had prayed for centuries *'next Year in Jerusalem'*, it seemed an impossible dream. Then it happened. Scripture was fulfilled. The Jewish people began to return to their homeland.

An Impossible Dream examines the historical events that happened and links them back to Scripture.

The Lloyd George cabinet of 1917 was predominately evangelical. Lord Balfour as Foreign Secretary was a strong believer. The letter he issued on November 2, 1917, known today as *'the Balfour Declaration'* announced British support for *"the establishment in Palestine of a national home for the Jewish people."*

A month later, General Allenby led British and Commonwealth forces into Jerusalem. The Ottoman Empire was defeated. As General Allenby entered Jerusalem, he dismounted from his horse and entered on foot, as a mark of respect for the city he was entering. Lloyd George called the victory 'A Christmas present for the British People'.

This book shows Scriptures and history coming together. **An Impossible Dream** by Gordon Pettie makes a fascinating read.

To order copies of this book please contact the Revelation TV office on +44 208 972 1400 or by emailing to infor@revelationtv.com